GREAT DAY
EVERY
DAY

NAVIGATING LIFE'S CHALLENGES
with PROMISE *and* PURPOSE

MAX LUCADO

THOMAS NELSON
Since 1798

NASHVILLE   DALLAS   MEXICO CITY   RIO DE JANEIRO

Published in Nashville, Tennessee, by Thomas Nelson. Thomas Nelson is a registered trademark of Thomas Nelson, Inc.

Thomas Nelson, Inc., titles may be purchased in bulk for educational, business, fund-raising, or sales promotional use. For information, please e-mail SpecialMarkets@ThomasNelson.com.

Unless otherwise noted, Scripture quotations are taken from *The Message* by Eugene H. Peterson. © 1993, 1994, 1995, 1996, 2000, 2001, 2002. Used by permission of NavPress Publishing Group. All rights reserved. Scripture quotations marked (CEV) are from the Contemporary English Version. © 1991 by the American Bible Society. Used by permission. Scripture quotations marked (GOD'S WORD) are from God's Word, a copyrighted work of God's Word to the Nations Bible Society. Quotations are used by permission. © 1995 by God's Word to the Nations Bible Society. All rights reserved. Scripture quotations marked (JB) are from *The Jerusalem Bible.* © 1966, 1967 and 1968 by Darton, Longman & Todd Ltd. and Doubleday & Company, Inc. Used by permission. Scripture quotations marked (NCV) are from the New Century Version®. © 2005 Thomas Nelson, Inc. Used by permission. All rights reserved. Scripture quotations marked (NIV) are from the Holy Bible, New International Version®, NIV®. © 1973, 1978, 1984 by Biblica, Inc.™ Used by permission of Zondervan. All rights reserved worldwide. Scripture quotations marked (NKJV) are from the New King James Version®. © 1982 by Thomas Nelson, Inc. Used by permission. All rights reserved. Scripture quotations marked (NLT) are from the Holy Bible, New Living Translation. © 1996, 2004, 2007. Used by permission of Tyndale House Publishers, Inc. Wheaton, Illinois 60189. All rights reserved. Scripture quotations marked (PHILLIPS) are from *J. B. Phillips: The New Testament in Modern English, Revised Edition.* © J. B. Phillips 1958, 1960, 1972. Used by permission of Macmillan Publishing Co., Inc. Scripture quotations marked (RSV) are from the Revised Standard Version of the Bible. © 1946, 1952, 1971, 1973 by the Division of Christian Education of the National Council of the Churches of Christ in the U.S.A. Used by permission. Scripture quotations marked (TLB) are from *The Living Bible.* © 1971. Used by permission of Tyndale House Publishers, Inc., Wheaton, Illinois 60189. All rights reserved. Scripture quotations marked (WEY) are from the Weymouth Bible.

ISBN 978-1-4041-8357-5 (IE)

Library of Congress Cataloging-in-Publication Data

Lucado, Max.
  Great day every day : navigating life's challenges with promise and purpose / Max Lucado.
    p. cm.
  Rev. ed. of: Every day deserves a chance.
  Includes bibliographical references (pp. 113–15).
  ISBN 978-0-8499-2073-8 (hardcover)
1. Christian life. I. Lucado, Max. Every day deserves a chance. II. Title.
  BV4501.3.L8175 2012
  248.4—dc23   2011037301

Printed in the United States of America

12 13 14 15 16 QG 5 4 3 2 1

To Vic and Kay King,
whose love for the least reminds me of His

CONTENTS

ACKNOWLEDGMENTS

Here are some friends who deserve a great day off after shepherding this book . . .

Liz Heaney and Karen Hill are to editors what Rolex is to watches—you make the pieces fit.

Steve and Cheryl Green—you set the standard for friendship.

Byron Williamson and Joey Paul—thanks for not thinking this idea was kooky.

Rob Birkhead—what creativity!

Jared Stephens—you went beyond the call of duty.

Carol Bartley—If it wusn't fur you, all my sintinces wud look lyke this!

The UpWords team—they don't come any better!

Jenna, Andrea, and Sara—you keep my heart in springtime.

And Denalyn, my wife—you make the grayest day explode with joy!

1

—◦◇◦—

EVERY DAY
DESERVES A CHANCE

S and soft to the feet, breeze cool on the skin. An apron of Pacific turquoise precedes one of deeper blue. Waves lap and slap. Birds whistle and coo. Islands loom on the horizon. Palm trees sway against the sky.

I found myself relishing the morning as I was writing this book. *What easier way to have a great day every day*, I mused, *than starting it right here?* I leaned back into a beach chair, interlaced my fingers behind my head, and closed my eyes.

That's when a bird chose my chest for target practice. No warning. No sirens. No "Bombs away!" Just *plop*.

I looked up just in time to see a seagull giving high feathers to his bird buddies on the branch. Yuck. I poured water on my shirt three times. I moved to a chair away from the trees. I did all I could to regain the magic of the morning, but I couldn't get my mind off the bird flyby.

It should have been easy. Waves still rolled. Clouds still floated. The ocean lost no blue; the sand lost no white. Islands still beckoned, and wind still whispered. But I couldn't quit thinking about the seagull grenade.

Stupid bird.

Birds have a way of messing things up, don't they? Count on it: into every day a bird will plop.

Traffic will snarl.

Airports will close.

Friends will forget.

Spouses will complain.

And lines. Oh, the lines. Deadlines, long lines, receding hairlines, luggage-losing airlines, nauseating pickup lines, wrinkle lines, unemployment lines, and those ever-elusive bottom lines.

And what of those days of double shadows? Those days when hope is Hindenberged by crisis? You never leave the hospital bed or wheelchair. You wake up and bed down in the same prison cell or war zone. The cemetery dirt is still fresh, the pink slip still folded in your pocket, the other side of the bed still empty . . . who has a good day on these days?

Most don't . . . but couldn't we try? Such days warrant an opportunity. A shot. A tryout. An audition. A swing at the plate. Doesn't every day deserve a chance to be a good day?

After all, "this is the day the LORD has made; we will rejoice and be glad in it" (Psalm 118:24 NKJV). The first word in the verse leaves us scratching our heads. "*This* is the day the LORD has made"? Perhaps holidays are the days the Lord has made. Wedding days are the days the Lord has made. Easter Sundays . . . super-sale Saturdays . . . vacation days . . . the first days of hunting season—these are the days the Lord has made. But "*this* is the day"?

"This is the day" includes every day. Divorce days, final-exam days, surgery days, tax days. Sending-your-firstborn-off-to-college days.

That last one sucked the starch out of my shirt. Surprisingly so. We packed Jenna's stuff, loaded up her car, and left life as we'd known it for eighteen years. A chapter was closing. One less plate on the table, voice in the house, and child beneath the roof. The day was necessary. The day was planned. But the day undid me.

I was a mess. I drove away from the gas station with the nozzle still in my tank, yanking the hose right off the pump. Got lost in a one-intersection town. We drove; I moped. We unpacked; I swallowed throat lumps. We filled the dorm room; I plotted to kidnap my own daughter and take her home where she belongs. Did someone store my chest in dry ice? Then I saw the verse. Some angel had tacked it to a dormitory bulletin board.

This is the day the Lord has made. We will rejoice and be glad in it.

I stopped, stared, and let the words sink in. God made this day, ordained this hard hour, designed the details of this wrenching moment. He isn't on holiday. He still holds the conductor's baton, sits in the cockpit, and occupies the universe's only throne. Each day emerges from God's drawing room. Including this one.

So I decided to give the day a chance, change my view, and imitate the resolve of the psalmist: "I will rejoice and be glad in it."

Oops, another word we'd like to edit: *in*. Perhaps we could swap it for *after*? We'll be glad after the day. Or *through*. We'll be glad to get through the day. *Over* would suffice. I'll rejoice when this day is over.

But rejoice *in* it? God invites us to. As Paul rejoiced *in* prison; David wrote psalms *in* the wilderness; Jonah prayed *in* the fish belly; Paul and Silas sang *in* jail; Shadrach, Meshach, and Abednego remained resolute *in* the fiery furnace; John saw heaven *in* his exile; and Jesus prayed *in* his garden of pain . . . Could we rejoice smack-dab *in* the midst of this day?

Imagine the difference if we could.

Suppose neck deep in a "terrible, horrible, no good, very bad day,"[1] you resolve to give it a chance. You choose not to drink or work or worry it away but give it a fair shake. You trust more. Stress less. Amplify gratitude. Mute grumbling. And what do you know? Before long the day is done and surprisingly decent.

So decent, in fact, that you resolve to give the next day the same fighting chance. It arrives with its hang-ups and bang-ups, bird drops and shirt stains, but by and large, by golly, giving the day a chance works! You do the same the next day and the next. Days become a week. Weeks become months. Months become years of good days.

In such a fashion good lives are built. One good day at a time.

An hour is too short, a year too long. Days are the bite-size portions of life, the God-designed segments of life management.

Eighty-four thousand heartbeats.

One thousand four hundred and forty minutes.

A complete rotation of the earth.

A circle of the sundial.

Two dozen flips of the hourglass.

Both a sunrise *and* a sunset.

A brand-spanking-new, unsoiled, untouched, uncharted, and unused day!

A gift of twenty-four unlived, unexplored hours.

And if you can stack one good day on another and another, you will link together a good life.

But here's what you need to keep in mind.

You no longer have yesterday. It slipped away as you slept. It is gone. You'll more easily retrieve a puff of smoke. You can't change, alter, or improve it. Sorry, no mulligans allowed. Hourglass sand won't flow upward. The second hand of the clock refuses to tick backward. The monthly calendar reads left to right, not right to left. You no longer have yesterday.

You do not yet have tomorrow. Unless you accelerate the orbit of the earth or convince the sun to rise twice before it sets once, you can't live tomorrow today. You can't spend tomorrow's money, celebrate tomorrow's achievements, or resolve tomorrow's riddles. You have only today. *This* is the day the Lord has made.

Live in it. You must be present to win. Don't heavy today with yesterday's regrets or acidize it with tomorrow's troubles. But don't we tend to do so?

We do to our day what I did to a bike ride. My friend and I went on an extended hill-country trek. A few minutes into the trip I began to tire. Within a half hour my thighs ached and my lungs heaved like a beached whale. I could scarcely pump the pedals. I'm no Tour de France contender, but neither am I a newcomer, yet I felt like one. After forty-five minutes I had to dismount and catch my breath. That's when my partner spotted the problem. Both rear brakes were rubbing my back tire! Rubber grips contested every pedal stroke. The ride was destined to be a tough one.

Don't we do the same? Guilt presses on one side. Dread drags the other. No wonder we weary so. We sabotage our day, wiring it for disaster, lugging along yesterday's troubles, downloading tomorrow's struggles. Remorse over the past, anxiety over the future. We aren't giving the day a chance.

How can we? What can we do? Here's my proposal: consult Jesus. The Ancient of Days has something to say about our days. He doesn't use the term *day* very often in Scripture. But the few times he does use it provide a delightful formula for upgrading each of ours to blue-ribbon status.

Saturate your day in his grace.
- "I tell you in solemn truth," replied Jesus, "that this very day you shall be with me in Paradise." (Luke 23:43 WEY)

Entrust your day to his oversight.
- "Give us day by day our daily bread." (Luke 11:3 NKJV)

Accept his direction.

- "If any of you want to be my followers, you must forget about yourself. You must take up your cross each day and follow me." (Luke 9:23 CEV)

Grace. Oversight. Direction.

- G-O-D

Fill your day with God. Give the day a chance. Choose to make it great. And while you are at it, keep an eye out for the seagull with the silly grin.

DAILY COMPASS

The next time you are mired in a bad day, check your outlook with these three questions:

1. What do I feel guilty about?
2. What am I worried about?
3. What am I about?

Reflect on your answers with these reminders:

Yesterday . . . forgiven.

Tomorrow . . . surrendered.

Today . . . clarified.

Jesus' design for a good day makes such sense. His grace
erases guilt. His oversight removes fear. His direction removes
confusion.

SECTION 1

◇◆◇

SATURATE YOUR DAY IN HIS GRACE

You messed up yesterday. You said the wrong words, took the wrong turn, loved the wrong person, reacted the wrong way. You spoke when you should have listened, walked when you should have waited, judged when you should have trusted, indulged when you should have resisted.

You messed up yesterday. But you'll mess up more if you let yesterday's mistakes sabotage today's attitude. God's mercies are new every morning. Receive them. Learn a lesson from the Cascade forests of Washington State. Some of its trees are hundreds of years old, far surpassing the typical life span of fifty to sixty years. One leaf-laden patriarch dates back seven centuries! What makes the difference? Daily drenching rains. Deluges keep the ground moist, the trees wet, and the lightning impotent.[1]

Lightning strikes you as well. Thunderbolts of regret can ignite and consume you. Counteract them with downpours of God's grace, daily washings of forgiveness. Once a year won't do. Once a month is insufficient. Weekly showers leave you dry. Sporadic mistings leave you combustible. You need a solid soaking every day. "The Lord's love never ends; his mercies never stop. They are new every morning" (Lamentations 3:22–23 NCV).

2

───◇◇◇───

MERCY FOR
SHAME-FILLED DAYS

What the thief sees. Dirty walls and a dingy floor. Rationed sunlight squeezing through cracks. The prison cell is shadowed. His day, more so. Rats scurry through corner holes. He'd do the same if he could.

What the thief hears. Soldiers' feet shuffling. A prison door clanging. A guard with the compassion of a black widow spider: "Get up! Your time has come."

What the thief sees. Defiant faces lining a cobbled path. Men spitting in disgust, women turning in derision. As the thief crests the top of the hill, a soldier yanks him down. Another presses his forearm against a beam and braces it with a knee. He sees the soldier reach for the mallet and spike.

What the thief hears. Pounding. Pounding hammer. Pounding head. Pounding heart. Soldiers grunt as they lift the cross. The base thuds as it falls into the hole.

What the thief feels. Pain. Breathtaking, pulse-stopping pain. Every fiber on fire.

What the thief hears. Groans. Guttural moans. Death. Nothing but. His own. Death. Golgotha plays it like a minor chord. No lullaby of hope. No sonnet of life. Just the harsh chords of death.

Pain. Death. He sees them; he hears them. But then the thief sees and hears something else: "Father, forgive them, for they do not know what they do" (Luke 23:34 NKJV).

A flute lilts on a battlefield. A rain cloud blocks the desert sun. A rose blossoms on death ridge.

Jesus prays on a Roman cross.

Here is how the thief reacts. Mockery. "Even the robbers who were crucified with Him reviled Him" (Matthew 27:44 NKJV).

Having been hurt, the thief hurts. Having been wounded, he wounds. Even Skull Hill has a pecking order, and this thief refuses the bottom rung. He joins the jeerers who are saying: "He saved others—he can't save himself! King of Israel, is he? Then let him get down from that cross. . . . He did claim to be God's Son, didn't he?" (Matthew 27:42–43).

But Jesus refuses to retaliate. The thief sees, for the first time that day (for the first time in how many days?), kindness. Not darting glances or snarling lips, but patient forbearance.

The thief softens. He stops mocking Christ and then attempts to stop the mocking of Christ. "We deserve this, but not him," he confesses to the crook on the other cross. "He did nothing to deserve this" (Luke 23:41). The thief senses he's close to a man heaven-bound and requests a recommendation: "Jesus, remember me when you enter your kingdom" (23:42).

And Jesus, who made and makes an eternal life out of inviting illegal immigrants into his Oval Office, issues this grace-drenched reply: "Don't worry, I will. Today you will join me in paradise" (Luke 23:43).

And the bad day of the bad man is met with the gracious gift of a mercy-giving God.

What does the thief see now? He sees a son entrust his mother to a friend and honor a friend with his mother (John 19:26–27). He sees the God who wrote the book on grace. The God who coaxed Adam and Eve out of the bushes, murderous Moses out of the desert. The God who made a place for David, though David made a move on Bathsheba. The God who didn't give up on Elijah, though Elijah gave up on God. This is what the thief sees.

What does he hear? He hears what fugitive Moses heard in the desert, depressed Elijah heard in the wilderness, adulterous David heard after Bathsheba. He hears what . . .

a fickle Peter heard after the rooster crowed,

the storm-tossed disciples heard after the wind stopped,

the cheating woman heard after the men left,

the oft-married Samaritan woman heard before the disciples came,

the hardheaded and hard-hearted Saul would hear after the light shone, the paralytic heard when his friends lowered him through the roof,

the blind man heard when Jesus found him on the street,

the disciples would soon hear from Jesus on the beach early one morning.

He hears the official language of Christ: grace. Undeserved. Unexpected. Grace. "Today you will join me in paradise" (Luke 23:43).

Paradise. The intermediate heaven. The home of the righteous until the return of Christ. The Tree of Life is there. Saints are there. God is there. And now the thief, who began the day in a Roman jail, will be there.

With Jesus. No back-door entrance. No late-night arrival. Paradise knows neither night nor second-class citizens. The thief enters the gate on Jesus' red carpet.

Today. Immediately. No Purgatory purging. No Hades rehab. Grace comes like a golden sunrise, illuminating the thief's dark day. Execution hill becomes a mount of transfiguration.

Perhaps you could use some of the same. Yesterday's mistakes play the role of the Roman death squad: they escort you up the calvary of shame. Faces of the past line the trail. Voices declare your crimes as you pass:

You neglected your father and me!

You let the habit rob your youth!

You promised you'd come back!

You're soon nailed to the cross of your mistakes. Dumb mistakes. What do you see? Death. What do you feel? Shame. What do you hear?

Ah, this is the question. What do you hear? Can you hear Jesus above the accusers? He promises, "Today you will join me in paradise."

Today. This day. In the stink of it, the throes of it, Jesus makes a miracle out of it. When others nail you to the cross of your past, he swings open the door to your future. Paradise. Jesus treats your shame-filled days with grace.

He'll take your guilt if you'll ask him. All he awaits is your request. The words of the thief will do. "We deserve this, but not him—he did nothing . . ."

We are wrong. He is right.

We sin. He is the Savior.

We need grace. Jesus can give it.

So ask him, "Remember me when you enter your kingdom."

And when you do, the one who spoke then will speak again. "Today you will join me in paradise."[1]

DAILY COMPASS

Next time your day goes south, here is what you do. Steep yourself in the grace of God. Saturate your day in his love. Marinate your mind in his mercy. He has settled your accounts, paid your debt. "Christ carried our sins in his body on the cross" (1 Peter 2:24 NCV).

When you lose your temper with your child, Christ intervenes: "I paid for that." When you tell a lie and all of heaven groans, your Savior speaks up: "My death covered that sin." As you lust, gloat, covet, or judge, Jesus stands before the tribunal of heaven and points to the blood-streaked cross. "I've already made provision. I've taken away the sins of the world."

What a gift he has given you. You've won the greatest lottery in the history of humanity, and you didn't even pay for the ticket! Your soul is secure, your salvation guaranteed. Your name is written in the only book that matters. You're only a few sand grains in the hourglass from a tearless, graveless, painless existence. What more do you need?

3

—◦◇◦—

GRATITUDE FOR UNGRATEFUL DAYS

Excerpts from the diary of a dog:

> 8:00 a.m. Oh boy, dog food—my favorite.
>
> 9:30 a.m. Oh boy, a car ride—my favorite.
>
> 9:40 a.m. Oh boy, a walk—my favorite.
>
> 10:30 a.m. Oh boy, another car ride—my favorite.
>
> 11:30 a.m. Oh boy, more dog food—my favorite.
>
> 12:00 p.m. Oh boy, the kids—my favorite.
>
> 1:00 p.m. Oh boy, the yard—my favorite.
>
> 4:00 p.m. Oh boy, the kids again—my favorite.
>
> 5:00 p.m. Oh boy, dog food again—my favorite.
>
> 5:30 p.m. Oh boy, Mom—my favorite.

6:00 p.m. Oh boy, playing ball—my favorite.

8:30 p.m. Oh boy, sleeping in my master's bed—my favorite.

Excerpts from the diary of a cat:

Day 283 of my captivity. My captors continue to taunt me with bizarre little dangling objects. They dine lavishly on fresh meat while I'm forced to eat dry cereal. I'm sustained by the hope of escape and the mild satisfaction I derive from ruining a few pieces of furniture. Tomorrow I may eat another houseplant. I attempted to kill my captors this morning by weaving through their walking feet. Nearly succeeded. Must try this strategy at the top of the stairs. Seeking to disgust and repulse these vile oppressors, I once again induced myself to vomit on their favorite chair. Must try this on their bed. To display my diabolical disposition, I decapitated a mouse and deposited the headless body on their kitchen floor. They only cooed and condescended, patting my head and calling me a "strong little kitty." Hmm—not working according to plan. During a gathering of their accomplices, they placed me in solitary confinement. I overheard that my confinement was due to my power of allergies. Must learn what this means and how to use it to my advantage.

I am convinced the other household captives are flunkies, perhaps snitches. The dog is routinely released and seems naively happy to return. He is, no doubt, a half-wit. The bird speaks with the humans regularly. Must be an informant. I am certain he reports my every move. Due to his current placement in the metal cage, his safety is assured, but I can wait. It is only a matter of time.[1]

———◇◇◇———

The day of a dog. The day of a cat. One content, the other conniving. One at peace, the other at war. One grateful, the other
grumpy. Same house. Same circumstances. Same master. Yet
two entirely different attitudes.

Which diary reads more like yours? Were your private
thoughts made public, how often would the phrase "Oh boy, my
favorite" appear?

"Oh boy, sunup—my favorite."

"Oh boy, breakfast—my favorite."

"Oh boy, traffic jam—my favorite."

"Oh boy, vacuuming—my favorite."

"Oh boy, root canal—my favorite."

Well, not even a dog would relish the root canal. But wouldn't
we like to relish more of our day? We can. Begin with God's
grace. As we accept his forgiveness, our day of gripes and groans
becomes a day of gratitude.

Yes, gratitude. Gratitude is the firstborn child of grace, the
appropriate response of the blessed. So appropriate, in fact, that
its absence surprises Jesus. We know this because of ten men he
healed.

"It happened that as he made his way toward Jerusalem,
he crossed over the border between Samaria and Galilee. As he
entered a village, ten men, all lepers, met him. They kept their
distance but raised their voices, calling out, 'Jesus, Master, have
mercy on us!'" (Luke 17:11–13).

Lepers. A huddle of half-draped faces and bent bodies. Who

could discern where one form stopped and the other began, they leaned on each other so? Yet upon whom else could they lean?

Their appearance repulsed people: lumps on the cheeks, nose, lips, and forehead. Ulcerated vocal cords rendered their voices a raspy wheeze. Hairless eyebrows turned eyes into hollow stares. Muscles atrophied and tendons contracted until hands looked like claws. People avoided lepers.

But Christ had compassion on them. So when people stepped back from the ten lepers, the Master stepped forward. "'Go, show yourselves to the priests.' They went, and while still on their way, became clean" (17:14).

Wouldn't you love to have witnessed the miracle? No therapy. No treatment. No medicine. Just one prayer to one man and *Pow!* Complete healing. Gnarled hands straightening. Open sores closing. Energy pulsating through veins. Ten hoods thrown back and twenty crutches dropped. A mass of misery becomes a leaping, jumping, celebrating chorus of health.

Can you imagine how the lepers felt? If you're in Christ, you can. What he did for the lepers physically, he has done for you spiritually.

Sin makes lepers of us all, turns us into spiritual corpses. To the Ephesian Christians, Paul wrote, "You were dead in your transgressions and sins" (Ephesians 2:1 NIV). The unsaved, Paul argued, live "in the futility of their thinking. They are darkened in their understanding and separated from the life of God" (Ephesians 4:17–18 NIV).

Could one render a more gloomy assessment?

Dead in transgressions.

Futile in thinking.

Darkened in understanding.

Separated from God.

Coroners give brighter reports. But Paul wasn't finished. Apart from Christ we are "without hope and without God" (Ephesians 2:12 NIV), "controlled by the sinful nature" (Romans 7:5 NIV), and slaves of Satan (2 Timothy 2:26). What Jesus saw in the lepers' bodies, he sees in the sinner's soul—utter devastation. But what he did for them, he does for the willing heart. "Because of his great love for us, God, who is rich in mercy, made us alive with Christ even when we were dead in transgressions" (Ephesians 2:4–5 NIV).

He closes the open sores of our hearts and straightens the gnarled limbs of our inner beings. He swaps sin rags for righteous robes. He still heals. And he still looks for gratitude.

When one of them saw that he was healed, he went back to Jesus, praising God in a loud voice. Then he bowed down at Jesus' feet and thanked him. (And this man was a Samaritan.) Jesus said, "Weren't ten men healed? Where are the other nine? Is this Samaritan the only one who came back to thank God?" (Luke 17:15–18 NCV)

The returning leper caught the attention of Christ. So did the absence of the others. Don't miss the headline of this story. God notices the grateful heart. Why? Does he have an ego problem? No. But we do. Gratitude lifts our eyes off the things we lack so we might see the blessings we possess. Nothing blows the winter out of the day like the Caribbean breeze of thankfulness. Need some trade winds?

Major in the grace of God. When Paul sent Timothy off to spiritual university, he told him to major in the grace of God: "You therefore, my son, *be strong in the grace* that is in Christ Jesus" (2 Timothy 2:1 NKJV, emphasis mine). Do the same. Focus on the cross of Christ. Grow fluent in the language of redemption. Linger long at the foot of the cross. Immerse yourself in the curriculum of grace. It's so easy to be distracted. So easy to be ungrateful, to make the mistake of Scott Simpson's caddie.

Scott is a professional golfer who plays often at the Masters Golf Tournament, hosted by the Augusta National Golf Club. Augusta National is to golfers what the Smithsonian is to history buffs: the ultimate experience. The course explodes in beauty. You would think you'd walked into an oil painting. Groomers manicure the course as if she's a wedding-day bride. In describing the perfection to his caddie, Scott commented, "You won't see a single weed all week."

Imagine Scott's surprise when, on Sunday, after five days of walking the course, his caddie pointed to the ground and announced to Scott, "I found one!"

Don't we do the same? We indwell a garden of grace. God's love sprouts around us like lilacs and towers over us like Georgia pines, but we go on weed hunts. How many flowers do we miss in the process?

If you look long enough and hard enough, you'll find something to bellyache about. So quit looking! Lift your eyes off the weeds. Major in the grace of God. And . . .

Measure the gifts of God. Collect your blessings. Catalog his kindnesses. Assemble your reasons for gratitude and recite them. "Always be joyful. Pray continually, and give thanks whatever happens. That is what God wants for you in Christ Jesus" (1 Thessalonians 5:16–18 NCV).

Look at the totality of those terms. *Always be joyful. Pray continually. Give thanks whatever happens.* Learn a lesson from Sidney Connell. When her brand-new bicycle was stolen, she called her dad with the bad news. He expected his daughter to be upset. But Sidney wasn't crying. She was honored. "Dad," she boasted, "out of all the bikes they could have taken, they took mine."

Gratitude is always an option. Matthew Henry made it his. When the famous scholar was accosted by thieves and robbed of his purse, he wrote this in his diary: "Let me be thankful first, because I was never robbed before; second, because, although they took my purse, they did not take my life; third, although they took my all, it was not much; and, fourthly, because it was I who was robbed, not I who robbed."[2]

Make gratitude your default emotion, and you'll find yourself giving thanks for the problems of life. Management consultant Robert Updegraff wrote:

> You ought to be glad for the troubles on your job because they provide about half your income. If it were not for the things that go wrong, the difficult people with whom you deal, and the problems of your working day, someone could be found to handle your job for half of what you are being paid. So start

looking for more troubles. Learn to handle them cheerfully and with good judgment, as opportunities rather than irritations, and you will find yourself getting ahead at a surprising rate. For there are plenty of big jobs waiting for people who are not afraid of troubles.[3]

Need spice in your day? Thank God for every problem that comes down the pike. Is any situation so dire that gratitude is eliminated? Some of the ladies at the Women of Faith Conference thought it was. This great organization fills arenas with women, and women with hope. The president, Mary Graham, told me about one particular weekend in which a shortage of space tested everyone's patience.

The floor had 150 fewer seats than needed. The arena staff tried to solve the problem by using narrow chairs. As a result, every woman had a place to sit, but everyone was crowded. Complaints contaminated like feedlot fragrance. Mary asked Joni Eareckson Tada, a speaker for the evening, if she could calm the crowd. Joni was perfectly qualified to do so. A childhood diving accident has left her wheelchair-bound. The attendants rolled her onto the platform, and Joni addressed the unhappy crowd. "I understand some of you don't like the chair in which you are sitting. Neither do I. But I have about a thousand handicapped friends who would gladly trade places with you in an instant."

The grumbling ceased.

Yours can too. Major in the grace of God. Measure the gifts of God. Who knows what you might record in your journal:

"Mondays, oh boy—my favorite."

"Tax days, oh boy—my favorite."

"Year-end-review day, oh boy—my favorite."

Impossible, you say? How do you know? How do you know until you give every day a chance?

DAILY COMPASS

Two types of voices command your attention today. Negative ones fill your mind with doubt, bitterness, and fear. Positive ones purvey hope and strength. Which ones will you choose to heed? You have a choice, you know. "We take every thought captive so that it is obedient to Christ" (2 Corinthians 10:5 GOD'S WORD).

Do you let anyone who knocks on your door enter your house? Don't let every thought that surfaces dwell in your mind. Take it captive . . . make it obey Jesus. If it refuses, don't think it.

Negative thoughts never strengthen you. How many times have you cleared a traffic jam with your grumbles? Does groaning about bills make them disappear? Why moan about your aches and pains, problems and tasks?

"Be careful what you think, because your thoughts run your life" (Proverbs 4:23 NCV).

4

---◦◇◦---

FORGIVENESS FOR
BITTER DAYS

You and I save things. Favorite photos, interesting articles . . . we all save things. Homer and Langley Collyer hoarded things. Everything. Newspapers, letters, clothing—you name it, they kept it.

Born in the late 1800s to an affluent Manhattan couple, the brothers lived in a luxurious, three-story mansion at the intersection of Fifth Avenue and 128th Street. Homer earned a degree in engineering; Langley became a lawyer. All seemed good in the Collyer family.

But then mom and dad divorced in 1909. The boys, now in their twenties, remained in the home with their mother. Crime escalated. The neighborhood deteriorated. Homer and Langley retaliated by escaping the world. For reasons that therapists discuss at dinner parties, the duo retreated into their inherited mansion, closed and locked the doors.

They were all but unheard of for nearly forty years. Then in 1947 someone reported the suspicion of a dead body at their address. It took seven policemen to break down the door. The entrance was blocked by a wall of newspapers, folding beds, half a sewing machine, old chairs, part of a winepress, and other pieces of junk. After several hours of digging, policemen found the body of Homer, seated on the floor, head between his knees, his long and matted gray hair reaching his shoulders.

But where was Langley? That question triggered one of the strangest searches in Manhattan history. Fifteen days of quarrying produced 103 tons of junk. Gas chandeliers, a sawhorse, the chassis of an old car, a Steinway piano, a horse's jawbone, and, finally, one missing brother. The stuff he'd kept had collapsed on and killed him.[1]

Bizarre! Who wants to live with yesterday's rubble? Who wants to hoard the trash of the past? You don't, do you?

Or do you?

Not in your house, mind you, but in your heart? Not the junk of papers and boxes but the remnants of anger and hurt. Do you pack-rat pain? Amass offenses? Record slights?

A tour of your heart might be telling. A pile of rejections stockpiled in one corner. Accumulated insults filling another. Images of unkind people lining the wall, littering the floor.

No one can blame you. Innocence takers, promise breakers,

wound makers—you've had your share. Yet doesn't it make sense to get rid of their trash? Want to give every day a chance? Jesus says, *Give the grace you've been given.*

Take a long look at his reply to Peter's question: "'Lord, how often should I forgive someone who sins against me? Seven times?' 'No, not seven times,' Jesus replied, 'but seventy times seven!'" (Matthew 18:21–22 NLT).

That noise you hear is the sound of clicking calculators. Seventy times seven equals four hundred and ninety offenses, we discover. *My, I can legally get rid of my husband. He blew past this number on our honeymoon.*

But then Jesus curtails our calibrated grace by relating a two-act play:

Act 1: *God forgives the unforgivable.*

> Therefore, the Kingdom of Heaven can be compared to a king who decided to bring his accounts up to date with servants who had borrowed money from him. In the process, one of his debtors was brought in who owed him millions of dollars. He couldn't pay, so his master ordered that he be sold—along with his wife, his children, and everything he owned—to pay the debt. (Matthew 18:23–25 NLT)

Such an immense debt. More literal translations say the servant owed 10,000 talents. One talent equaled 6,000 denarii. One denarius equaled one day's wage (Matthew 20:2). One talent, then, would equate to 6,000 days' worth of work. Ten thousand talents would represent 60 million days or 240,000 years of labor. A person earning $100 a day would owe $6 billion.

Whoa! What an astronomical sum. Jesus employs hyperbole, right? He's exaggerating to make a point. Or is he? One person would never owe such an amount to another. But might Jesus be referring to the debt we owe to God?

Let's calculate our indebtedness to him. How often do you sin, hmm, in an hour? To sin is to "fall short" (Romans 3:23 NIV). Worry is falling short on faith. Impatience is falling short on kindness. The critical spirit falls short on love. How often do you come up short with God? For the sake of discussion, let's say ten times an hour and tally the results. Ten sins an hour, times sixteen waking hours (assuming we don't sin in our sleep), times 365 days a year, times the average male life span of seventy-four years. I'm rounding the total off at 4,300,000 sins per person.

Tell me, how do you plan to pay God for your 4.3 million sin increments? Your payout is unachievable. Unreachable. You're swimming in a Pacific Ocean of debt. Jesus' point precisely. The debtor in the story? You and me. The king? God. Look at what God does.

> He [the servant] couldn't pay, so his master ordered that he be sold—along with his wife, his children, and everything he owned—to pay the debt. But the man fell down before his master and begged him, "Please be patient with me, and I will pay it all." Then his master was filled with pity for him, and he released him and forgave his debt. (Matthew 18:25–27 NLT)

God pardons the zillion sins of selfish humanity. Forgives sixty million sin-filled days. "Out of sheer generosity he put us in right standing with himself. A pure gift. He got us out of the mess we're in and restored us to where he always wanted us to be. And he did it by means of Jesus Christ" (Romans 3:24).

God forgives the unforgivable. Were this the only point of the story, we'd have ample points to ponder. But this is only Act 1 of the two-act play. The punch line is yet to come.

Act 2: We do the unthinkable.

The forgiven refuse to forgive.

> But when the man left the king, he went to a fellow servant who owed him a few thousand dollars. He grabbed him by the throat and demanded instant payment. His fellow servant fell down before him and begged for a little more time. "Be patient with me, and I will pay it," he pleaded. But his creditor wouldn't wait. He had the man arrested and put in prison until the debt could be paid in full. (Matthew 18:28–30 NLT)

Incomprehensible behavior. Multimillion-dollar forgiveness should produce a multimillion-dollar forgiver, shouldn't it? The forgiven servant can forgive a petty debt, can't he? This one doesn't. Note, he won't wait (18:30). He refuses to forgive. He could have. He should have. The forgiven should forgive. Which makes us wonder, did this servant truly accept the king's forgiveness?

Something is missing from this story. Gratitude. Notably absent from the parable is the joy of the forgiven servant. Like the nine ungrateful lepers we read about in the last chapter, this man never tells the king "thank you." He offers no words of appreciation, sings no song of celebration. His life has been spared, family liberated, sentence lifted, titanic debt forgiven—and he says nothing. He should be hosting a Thanksgiving Day parade. He begs for mercy like a student on the brink of flunking out of college. But once he receives it, he acts as if he never scored less than a B.

Could his silence make the loudest point of the parable? "He who is forgiven little, loves little" (Luke 7:47 RSV). This man loves little apparently because he had received little grace.

You know who I think this guy is? A grace rejecter. He never accepts the grace of the king. He leaves the throne room with a sly smirk, as one who dodged a bullet, found a loophole, worked the system, pulled a fast one. He talked his way out of a jam. He bears the mark of the unforgiven—he refuses to forgive.

When the king hears about the servant's stingy heart, he blows his crown. He goes cyclonic:

> "You wicked servant! I forgave you all that debt because you begged me. Should you not also have had compassion on your fellow servant, just as I had pity on you?" And his master was angry, and delivered him to the torturers until he should pay all that was due to him. So My heavenly Father also will do to you if each of you, from his heart, does not forgive his brother his trespasses. (Matthew 18:32–35 NKJV)

The curtain falls on Act 2, and we are left to ponder the principles of the story. The big one comes quickly. *The grace-given give grace*. Forgiven people forgive people. The mercy-marinated drip mercy. "God is kind to you so you will change your hearts and lives" (Romans 2:4 NCV).

We are not like the unchanged wife. Before her conversion to Christ, she endlessly nagged, picked on, and berated her husband. When she became a Christian, nothing changed. She kept nagging. Finally he told her, "I don't mind that you were born again. I just wish you hadn't been born again as yourself."

One questions if the wife was born again to start with. Apple trees bear apples, wheat stalks produce wheat, and forgiven people forgive people. Grace is the natural outgrowth of grace.

The forgiven who won't forgive can expect a sad fate—a life full of many bad and bitter days. The "master . . . delivered him to the torturers until he should pay all that was due to him" (Matthew 18:34 NKJV).

Hoard hurts in your heart and expect the joy level of a Siberian death camp. A friend shared with me the fate of a hoarding grandmother. Like the Collyer brothers, she refused to part with anything. Her family witnessed two terrible consequences: she lost sleep and treasures. She couldn't rest because junk covered her bed. She lost treasures because they were obscured by mountains of trash. Jewelry, photographs, favorite books—all were hidden.

No rest. No treasures. Squirrel away your hurts and expect the same.

Or clean your house and give the day a fresh chance!

"But, Max, the hurt is so deep."

I know. They took much. Your innocence, your youth, your retirement. But why let them keep taking from you? Haven't they stolen enough? Refusing to forgive keeps them loitering, taking still.

"But, Max, what they did was so bad."

You bet it was. Forgiveness does not mean approval. You aren't endorsing misbehavior. You are entrusting your offender to "Him who judges righteously" (1 Peter 2:23 NKJV).

"But, Max, I've been so angry for so long."

And forgiveness won't come overnight. But you can take baby steps in the direction of grace. Forgive in phases. Quit cussing the perpetrator's name. Start praying for him. Try to understand her situation.

Let Antwone Fisher inspire you. He had ample reason to live with a cluttered heart. For the first thirty-three years of his life, he knew neither of his parents. His father had died before Antwone was born. And his mother, for reasons that he longed to know, abandoned him as a boy. He grew up as a foster child in Cleveland, abused, neglected, and desperate to find a single member of his family.

Equipped with the name of his father and a Cleveland phone book, he began calling people of the same last name. His life changed the day an aunt answered the phone. He told her his date of birth and his father's identity. He described the difficult turns his life had taken: being kicked out by his foster mom, serving a stint in the navy, now holding his own as a security guard in Los Angeles.

Her voice was warm. "You have a big family." Before long another aunt invited him to Cleveland for a Thanksgiving reunion and filled the week with a lifetime of belated love.

And then, after days of calls and attempts, his family found his mother's brother. He offered to take Antwone to the housing project where she lived. On the drive Antwone rehearsed the questions he'd longed to ask for the last three decades:

Why didn't you come for me?

Didn't you ever wonder about me?

Didn't you miss me at all?

But the questions were never uttered. The door opened, and Antwone walked into a dimly lit apartment with shabby furniture. Turning, he saw a frail woman who looked too old to be his mother. Her hair was uncombed. She wore her nightclothes.

Antwone's uncle said to her, "This is Antwone Quenton Fisher." Antwone's mother made the connection and started to moan, losing her footing, holding on to a chair. "Oh, God, please . . . Oh, God." She turned her face away in shame and hurried out of the room, crying.

Antwone learned that his mother had tried to get a man to marry her so she could raise her son, but couldn't. She had gone on to bear four other children, also raised as wards of the state. Over the years she'd been hospitalized, incarcerated, and put on probation. And when he realized how painful her years had been, he chose to forgive.

He writes, "Though my road had been long and hard, I finally understood that my mother's had been longer and harder. . . . Where the hurt of abandonment had lived inside me, now there was only compassion."[2]

In the end, we all choose what lives inside us.

May you choose forgiveness.

DAILY COMPASS

Here's God's agenda for your day: to make you more like Jesus.

"God . . . decided from the outset to shape the lives of those who love him along the same lines as the life of his Son" (Romans 8:29). Do you see what God is doing? Shaping you "along the same lines as the life of his Son."

Jesus felt no guilt; God wants you to feel no guilt.

Jesus had no bad habits; God wants to do away with yours.

Jesus faced fears with courage; God wants you to do the same.

Jesus knew the difference between right and wrong; God wants us to know the same.

Jesus served others and gave his life for the lost; we can do likewise.

Jesus dealt with anxiety about death; you can too.

God's desire, his plan, his ultimate goal is to make you into the image of Christ.

SECTION 2

—◇—

ENTRUST YOUR DAY TO HIS OVERSIGHT

I n one of my not-so-bright moments, I entered a race that began with a 1.2–mile ocean swim. Six hundred of us gathered on the beach at sunrise, some hoping to win a medal. I was hoping to finish before dinner. Six orange buoys silhouetted our path. My swimming buddies had told me the key to staying on track: every four or five strokes lift your head out of the water and get your bearings. The last thing you want to do is drift off course and swim extra distance.

Sounded simple. I'd executed the "lift and look" exercise to perfection in the swimming pool. But in the wind-chopped ocean?

Did I mention wind-chopped? We collectively gulped as the flag above stretched straighter and the gales blew harder. Gusts were transforming the bay into a salt-crested mountain range. What's worse, the wind blew south. We were swimming north. "No problem," I coached myself. "Just swim from buoy to buoy."

Within minutes my "buoy to buoy" became "boy oh boy." This minnow stood no chance. Every time I lifted and looked, I saw nothing but the next wave. It was a disaster. For all I knew, I was swimming in circles.

Then all of a sudden help swam over me. Half a dozen swimmers made an overpass out of my body. Initially, I was aggravated. Then I realized, *They know where they are going*, and joined up. How much easier. No searching the waves for bobbing markers; just stay with the gang. So I did. We glided through the bay with dolphin confidence, logging in a good ten minutes, each stroke bringing us closer to the end.

Then my hand slapped the rescue canoe. I stopped and looked up at the race official. One by one, my newfound water buddies swam into my back or the boat. Midwater pileup.

"Where you folks headed?" asked the canoe guy. For the first time in some time, I looked around. We were at least a quarter mile off track, right on target to reach China. We looked at each other. No one said it, but I know we all thought it. I sure did. *I thought you guys knew where we were going.*

So many swimmers couldn't be wrong, could we? Yes, we could.

A bit ticked and more embarrassed, we turned toward the shore and rejoined the event. I wasn't the last one out of the water, but I could see her behind me.

Ever have days like that? Days when you suddenly realize you're way off track or out of whack? God sends a rescue boat into such days. Jesus, positioned higher than the waves and enjoying a clear view of the shoreline, offers us his oversight: "Need help getting back on course?"

Wise are the ones who nod and swim in the direction he points.

5

---◇---

PEACE FOR ANXIOUS DAYS

Let's make a list. *The advantages of anxiety.* We have so many opportunities to practice. Just look at the front page of any newspaper.

I did. I began preparing this chapter on April 11. As a test, I searched the headlines of that date for ulcer makers. Not a recommended exercise. One article described a war on the other side of the world. In another, critics questioned the president's strategy and decisions. Politicians were demanding the resignation of a military leader. An Asian military base was attacked.

As if global conflicts weren't enough, personal tragedies abounded. A forty-year-old lieutenant colonel had died of a heart attack a week after buying his retirement farm. A salesman slid off the road in his car, and he was severely wounded. Another rural pasture was sacrificed on the altar of progress as the city issued a building permit to a developer.

What depressing headlines! War. A bombed base. Heart attacks. Car wrecks. Urban sprawl. Wring your hands and swallow your antacids. Fretting is the logical response to such chaos. So let's start making the list.

Here's the first entry: *worry helps our health*. Lose sleep and live longer. A nervous stomach is a happy stomach, isn't it? Actually, no. Worry has been cited for a swarm of sicknesses: heart trouble, high blood pressure, rheumatism, ulcers, colds, thyroid malfunction, arthritis, migraine headaches, blindness, and a host of stomach disorders.[1] Worry hurts our health. But at least worry makes us feel better.

Worry brings joy. Worry puts the blue in the sky, the spring in the step, and the song in the bird. A dose of fret spices up the day, right? For that reason we plan "worry vacations." Others camp, fish, shop, or sightsee. You and I plan seven days of worry.

Monday: stress out over the economy.

Tuesday: dread next year's workload.

Wednesday: enumerate all the communicable diseases to which we are vulnerable.

Thursday: list the reasons we could be unemployed by year's end.

Friday: calculate the number of ways to die on an airplane.

Saturday: envision life after a car accident, and

Sunday: record all the characteristics people don't like in us. First entry? Worrywart.

You don't do this? You don't sunbathe on the shores of the Sea of Dread? Oops. It appears I've confused the terms. We prefer worry-free not worry-*full* vacations. Worry is to joy what a Hoover vacuum cleaner is to dirt: might as well attach your heart to a happiness-sucker and flip the switch.

Let's keep thinking. Surely anxiety has some value. Even if it takes health and steals joy, doesn't worry usher in some blessing? How about this one: *worry solves our problems*? Treat your troubles to a good dose of fretting and watch them evaporate. Correct?

Wrong again. Remember the headlines I cited? The war on the other side of the world. Political sabotage. Urban issues, heart attacks, and car wrecks. I gave you the date of the paper: April 11. I failed to mention the year of the publication: 1956. The war was the Korean War. The dismissed military leader was Douglas MacArthur. Heart attacks, car wrecks, and urban challenges— our parents and grandparents worried about them too.

Their anxiety didn't end the problems. Ours won't either. Let's face it. Anxiety has no advantages. It ruins health, robs joy, and changes nothing.

Our days stand no chance against the terrorists of the Land of Anxiety. But Christ offers a worry-bazooka. Remember how he taught us to pray? "Give us day by day our daily bread" (Luke 11:3 NKJV).

This simple sentence unveils God's provision plan: *live one day at a time.* God disclosed the strategy to Moses and the Israelites in the wilderness. Heaven knew they needed it. The freed slaves had taken anxiety to a new art form. You'd think they would have given seminars on faith. They had witnessed the plagues, walked on dry ground through the Red Sea, and watched the Egyptian soldiers drown. They had beheld one miracle after another, but still they worried: "The whole community of Israel complained about Moses and Aaron. 'If only the Lord had killed us back in Egypt,' they moaned. 'There we sat around pots filled with meat and ate all the bread we wanted. But now you have brought us into this wilderness to starve us all to death'" (Exodus 16:2–3 NLT).

Wait a minute. Are these the same people the Egyptians beat and overworked? The same Hebrews who cried to God for deliverance? And now, just a month into freedom, they speak as if Egypt were a paid vacation. They've forgotten. They've forgotten the miracles they saw and the misery they knew.

Forgetfulness sires fretfulness.

But God, patient as he is with memory loss, sends reminders. "Then the Lord said to Moses, 'Look, I'm going to rain down food from heaven for you. Each day the people can go out and pick up as much food as they need for that day. I will test them in this to see whether or not they will follow my instructions. On the sixth day they will gather food, and when they prepare it, there will be twice as much as usual'" (16:4–5 NLT).

Note the details of God's provision plan.

He meets daily needs daily. Quail covered the compound in the evenings; manna glistened like fine frost in the mornings. Meat for dinner. Bread for breakfast. The food fell every day. Not annually, monthly, or hourly, but daily. And there is more.

He meets daily needs miraculously. When the people first saw the wafers on the ground, "the Israelites took one look and said to one another, *man-hu* (What is it?). They had no idea what it was" (16:15).

The stunned people named the wafers *man-hu*, Hebrew for "What in the world is this?" God had resources they knew nothing about, solutions outside their reality, provisions outside their possibility. They saw the scorched earth; God saw heaven's breadbasket. They saw dry land; God saw a covey of quail behind every bush. They saw problems; God saw provision.

Anxiety fades as our memory of God's goodness doesn't.

When my daughters were single-digit ages—two, five, and seven—I wowed them with a miracle. I told them the story of Moses and the manna and invited them to follow me on a wilderness trek through the house.

"Who knows," I suggested, "manna may fall from the sky again."

We dressed in sheets and sandals and did our best Bedouin hike through the bedrooms. The girls, on my instruction, complained to me, Moses, of hunger and demanded I take them back to Egypt, or at least to the kitchen. When we entered the den, I urged them to play up their parts: groan, moan, and beg for food.

"Look up," I urged. "Manna might fall at any minute."

Two-year-old Sara obliged with no questions, but Jenna and Andrea had their doubts. How can manna fall from a ceiling?

Just like the Hebrews. "How can God feed us in the wilderness?"

Just like you? You look at tomorrow's demands, next week's bills, next month's silent calendar. Your future looks as barren as the Sinai Desert. "How can I face my future?" God tells you what I told my daughters: "Look up."

When my daughters did, manna fell! Well, not manna, but vanilla wafers dropped from the ceiling and landed on the carpet. Sara squealed with delight and started munching. Jenna and Andrea were old enough to request an explanation.

My answer was simple. I knew the itinerary. I knew we would enter this room. Vanilla wafers fit safely on the topside of the ceiling-fan blades. I had placed them there in advance. When they groaned and moaned, I turned on the switch.

God's answer to the Hebrews was similar. Did he know their itinerary? Did he know they would grow hungry? Yes and yes. And at the right time, he tilted the manna basket toward earth.

And what about you? God knows what you need and where you'll be. Any chance he has some vanilla wafers on tomorrow's ceiling fans? Trust him. "Give your entire attention to what God is doing right now, and don't get worked up about what may or may not happen tomorrow. God will help you deal with whatever hard things come up when the time comes" (Matthew 6:34).

The Greek word for worry, *merimnao*, stems from the verb *merizo* (divide) and the noun *nous* (mind). Worry cleaves the mind, splitting thoughts between today and tomorrow. Today stands no chance against it. Fretting over tomorrow's problems today siphons the strength you need for now, leaving you anemic and weak.

Worry gives small problems big shadows. Montaigne said, "My life has been full of terrible misfortunes, most of which never happened."[2] Corrie ten Boom commented, "Worry does not empty tomorrow of its sorrows; it empties today of its strength."[3] Worry scuttles our lives, hurts us, and most sadly, dishonors God.

God says: "Every detail in our lives of love for God is worked into something good" (Romans 8:28).

Worry takes a look at catastrophes and groans, "It's all coming unraveled."

God's Word says, "[God has] done it all and done it well" (Mark 7:37).

Worry disagrees: "The world has gone crazy."

God's Word calls God "the blessed controller of all things" (1 Timothy 6:15 PHILLIPS).

Worry wonders if anyone is in control.

God's Word declares, "God will take care of everything you need" (Philippians 4:19).

Worry whispers this lie: "God doesn't know what you need."

God's Word reasons: "You're at least decent to your own children. So don't you think the God who conceived you in love will be even better?" (Matthew 7:11).

Worry discounts and replies, "You're on your own. It's you against the world."

Worry wages war on your faith. You know that. You hate to worry. But what can you do to stop it? These three worry stoppers deserve your consideration:

Pray more. No one can pray and worry at the same time. When we worry, we aren't praying. When we pray, we aren't worrying. "You will keep him in perfect peace, whose mind is stayed on You, because he trusts in You" (Isaiah 26:3 NKJV).

When you pray, you "stay" your mind on Christ, resulting in peace. Bow your knees and banish anxiety.

Want less. Most anxiety stems, not from what we need, but

from what we want. As Charles Spurgeon penned more than a century ago,

> Enough for today is all we can enjoy. We cannot eat or drink or wear more than today's supply of food and clothing. The surplus gives us the care of storing it and the anxiety that someone might steal it. One staff aids a traveler; a bunch of staves is a heavy burden. Enough is as good as a feast and more than gluttony can enjoy. Enough is all we should expect, but a craving for more is ungratefulness. When our Father does not give you more, be content with your daily allowance.[4]

"Delight yourselves in the Lord, yes, find your joy in him at all times" (Philippians 4:4 PHILLIPS). If God is enough for you, then you'll always have enough, because you'll always have God.

Live for today. Heaven still has her manna house. The bushes still hide quail. And you still have today. Don't sacrifice it on the altar of anxiety. "Live only for the hour and its allotted work. . . . Set earnestly at the little task at your elbow . . . our plain duty is 'not to see what lies dimly at a distance, but to do what lies clearly at hand.'"[5]

May I urge you to do the same? "Go confidently to the throne of God's kindness to receive mercy and find kindness, which will help us at *the right time*" (Hebrews 4:16 GOD'S WORD, emphasis mine).

Some of my friends saw an example of God's perfect timing during a trip to Natal, Brazil. They were conducting a children's seminar at a delightful congregation called Refugio da Graca.

The church is situated five minutes from a tall bridge that has become infamous for suicide attempts. So many people have taken their lives by jumping from the structure that the church held a prayer vigil specifically for the bridge. Their prayers saw fruit when my friends were walking past at the very moment a woman was about to jump. She had climbed over the railing and was only a step from death. With much persuasion and effort, they talked her back from the ledge and saved her life.

Remarkably, their walk across the bridge was not in their original plan. They had been eating lunch at a restaurant and needed to return to the church building for the afternoon session. But the person scheduled to pick them up was late; hence, they chose to walk back. Their host was tardy, but God was right on time.

Isn't he always? He sends help at the hour we need it.

You don't have wisdom for tomorrow's problems. But you will tomorrow. You don't have resources for tomorrow's needs. But you will tomorrow. You don't have courage for tomorrow's challenges. But you will when tomorrow comes.

What you do have is manna for the morning and quail for the evening: bread and meat for the day. God meets daily needs daily and miraculously. He did then, he does still, and he will for you.

DAILY COMPASS

An accomplished Ironman triathlete told me the secret of his success. "You last the long race by running short ones." Don't swim 2.4 miles; just swim to the next buoy. Rather than bike 112 miles, ride 10, take a break, and bike 10 more. Never tackle more than the challenge ahead.

Didn't Jesus offer the same counsel? "So don't ever worry about tomorrow. After all, tomorrow will worry about itself. Each day has enough trouble of its own" (Matthew 6:34 GOD'S WORD).

When asked how he managed to write so many books, Joel Henderson explained that he'd never written a book. All he did was write one page a day.[6] Face challenges in stages. You can't control your temper forever, but you can control it for the next hour. Earning a college degree can seem impossible, but studying one semester is manageable, and logging in one good week is doable. You last the long race by running the short ones.

6

HOPE FOR
CATASTROPHIC DAYS

Vanderlei de Lima. He's just a whisper of a guy. At five feet five inches, he stands shorter than some fifth graders. At 119 pounds, he should be eligible for discount airline tickets. But don't let the size of the little Brazilian fool you. The body may be small, but the heart is bigger than the Olympic Stadium in Athens. That's where he received the 2004 bronze medal for the marathon.

He should have won the gold. He was leading the race with only three miles to go when a spectator accosted him. A deranged protester from Ireland, who had been imprisoned for running on a Grand Prix racetrack in England a year earlier, hurled himself into the runner, forcing him off the course and into the crowd.

Although stunned and shaken, de Lima collected himself and resumed the race. In the process he lost his rhythm, precious seconds, and his position.

But he never lost his joy. The small-bodied, big-hearted Brazilian entered the old marble stadium with the thrill of a child. He punched the air with his fists, then ran with both arms extended, like a human airplane looking for a place to land, weaving for joy.

Later, crowned with an olive wreath and bejeweled with an unflappable smile, he explained his exhilaration: "It is a festive moment. It is a unique moment. Most athletes never have this moment."

Yeah, but most athletes never get bumped off the path either.

Vanderlei de Lima never complained. "The Olympic spirit prevailed again. . . . I was able to medal for myself and my country."[1]

I'm taking notes on this guy. Wondering how de Lima kept such an attitude. Race bumpers still prowl the crowds. You don't have to run a marathon to go from the front of the pack to flat on your back. Just ask the kids who gather at their mom's grave. Or the patients waiting their turn for cancer therapy. Cemetery. Chemotherapy. The spouse who moved out, the soldier who returns missing a limb, the parents of the runaway daughter, the family made homeless by the hurricane.

Life catastrophically derailed. How do you get back in the race?

Let's turn to another runner for a few ideas. Take a look at him. Peer through the small window in the wall of the Roman jail. See the man in chains? The aging fellow with the stooped shoulders and hawkish nose? That's Paul, the imprisoned apostle. His chains never come off. The guards never leave. And he's probably wondering if he'll ever get out.

Bumped off track. Trouble began a couple of years earlier in Jerusalem. Though Paul went out of his way to pacify the Jewish scruples, religious leaders accused him of blasphemy. They nearly killed him and then unfairly imprisoned him. They maligned his name, violated his rights, and disrupted his plans.

His Roman citizenship saved his neck. Entitled to a Roman hearing, he journeyed from Jerusalem to Rome. No Mediterranean cruise. Paul survived a hurricane only to be bitten by a snake, the snakebite only to be stranded on an island for three months. When he was finally delivered to Rome, his case languished for two years in the bowels of a bureaucratic monster called the Roman empire.

By the time we find Paul in his cell, he has been beaten, lied about, storm tossed, rejected, and neglected.

Ah, but at least he has the church. At least he can take comfort in the thought of the unified Roman congregation he helped strengthen, right? Hardly. The Roman church is in trouble. From the jail cell, the apostle writes, "Some indeed preach Christ from envy and rivalry. . . . [They] proclaim Christ out of partisanship, not sincerely but thinking to afflict me in my imprisonment" (Philippians 1:15, 17 RSV).

Power-hungry preachers occupy the parsonage. You expect such antics out of nonbelievers, but Christians preaching for personal gain? Paul is facing Prozac-level problems.

And who knows what Emperor Nero will do? He feeds disciples to the lions for lunch. Does Paul have any guarantee the same won't happen to him? His prison-epistle word selection suggests he doesn't: "whether I live or die" (1:20 NCV). Then soon after, "dying would be profit for me" (1:21 NCV). Paul is not naive. He knows the only thing between him and death is a nod from moody Nero.

Paul has every reason to be stressed out.

So do you. You, like Paul, have been bumped off track, incarcerated in the sum total of your bad breaks. Each brick is a mishap. Each bar a rotten deal. And chained next to you is not a Roman guard but a diligent cohort of Lucifer's, whose sole assignment is to stir the sour soup of self-pity. "Just look at all the bad things that have happened to you." He has a point. No one questions the fact of your misfortunes. But one would wisely question the wisdom of rehearsing them.

Paul doesn't. Rather than count the bricks of his prison, he plants a garden within it. He itemizes not the mistreatments of people but the faithfulness of God.

"I want you to know, brethren" (Philippians 1:12 NKJV). This phrase is Paul's way of highlighting a paragraph. He uses it elsewhere to headline his points.[2] In this case, it is important for the Philippians to know "that what has happened to me has really served to advance the gospel" (1:12 NIV).

Have you ever lost your voice but not your health? You sound hoarse but still feel as healthy as one? People sympathize with your illness only to hear you whisper, "I really feel fine. It may appear that I am sick, but really . . ."

Paul is saying the same. He may appear to be bumped off track, but he is actually right on target. Why? One reason. Christ is preached. The mission is being accomplished. "It has become known throughout the whole praetorian guard and to all the rest that my imprisonment is for Christ" (1:13 RSV).

The praetorian guard was a handpicked division of crack imperial troops. They received double pay and added benefits. They were the finest of the fine. And, in God's sovereignty, the finest of Caesar's soldiers are chained to the finest of God's. How much time passed before Paul realized what was happening? How long before Paul looked at the chains, looked at the bright West Point graduate, and then smiled a smile toward heaven? *Hmm. Captive audience.* He leans toward the soldier. "Got a minute to talk?" Or "Would you mind proofreading this letter I'm writing?" or "Can I tell you about a Jewish carpenter I know?"

His words meet their mark. Read this line from the Philippian benediction: "All of God's people greet you, particularly those from the palace of Caesar" (4:22 NCV).

The man may be manacled, but the message is not. The prison of Paul becomes the pulpit of Paul, and that is fine with him. Any method is fine as long as Christ is preached.

And any motive is fine as long as Christ is preached. Remember the problem with the preachers? "Some indeed preach Christ from envy and rivalry . . . partisanship" (1:15, 17 RSV). Paul says they are "wanting to make trouble for me in prison" (1:17 NCV).

Who are these preachers? Ginsu-tongued stirrers of strife. Exactly the kind of folks you'd think would give the imprisoned Paul heartburn.

Not so. Paul is not worried about them; he is thankful for them. "The important thing is that in every way, whether for right or wrong reasons, they are preaching about Christ" (1:18 NCV).

Few passages in Scripture are punctuated with such faith. Paul displays absolute trust in God's oversight. So what if someone preaches from poor motives? Is God not greater than his people? He trumps bad preachers. The power is in the author's hand, not the pen he holds.

Knowing this, Paul can write from the chill of the jail, "So I am happy, and I will continue to be happy" (1:18 NCV).

Unfairly arrested. Unkindly treated. Uncharted future. Yet unbridled joy.

Bumped off track but still in the race. How? We can summarize all the reasons with one word. Reduce all the answers to a single verb. Distill the explanations into one decision. What is the word, verb, and decision?

Trust.

Paul trusted the oversight of God. He didn't know why bad things happened. He didn't know how they would be resolved. But he knew who was in charge.

Knowing who's in charge counterbalances the mystery of why and how. Such was the discovery of a Hungarian Jew I met in Jerusalem.

Joseph didn't fit the prototype of a greeter. He didn't smell good. His salt-and-pepper beard seemed to reach his waist. A woolen hat contained his wiry hair. He'd lost more teeth than he'd kept. Other churches might have placed someone else at the front door of the church. But the Netivya congregation didn't. They knew his story and loved to retell it.

As Hitler ravaged eastern Europe decades earlier, Joseph was captured and imprisoned in a concentration camp. As he and hundreds of others were marched to the prison, he spotted a book protruding from the pocket of a dead Jew lying on the side of the road. He snatched and hid it, only later realizing it was a New Testament. He was able to read most of it before a guard at the camp took it from him.

After several months of unspeakable horrors, he escaped and eked out an existence in the woods for two years. At one point the hunger and cold compromised his better judgment, and he knocked on the door of a farmhouse, looking for food. He had no way of knowing an SS party was taking place within.

The Nazi officer who answered the door knew in a moment that Joseph was an escaped prisoner. He stepped onto the porch and closed the door behind him. "Do you know who I am?"

Joseph could only muster a meek "I am hungry."

The soldier placed a gun to Joseph's head. "Do you know what I could do to you?"

Joseph could only reply, "I am hungry."

After what seemed to Joseph like an eternity, the German holstered his pistol. "Hitler is a thousand miles from here, and he'll never know what I do." He entered the house and returned with a basket of food.

Joseph knew someone was protecting him.

After the war he made his way to Israel. The cruelty had exacted a high cost on his mind; he had trouble eating, carrying on a conversation, keeping a job. In many ways he checked out of civilization. Sometime in the early 1960s, a hitchhiking Joseph was given a ride by a Christian minister—Joe Shulam. When Joseph spotted a New Testament on the dash of the minister's car, he remembered the one he'd smuggled into the camp and asked to hear about Jesus. He said he wouldn't leave the car until he'd heard the entire story. The minister gladly obliged, and Joseph realized that Jesus had swayed the heart of the Nazi officer on that porch years before.

Joseph chose to follow Christ. Shulam took him to the church, and Joseph never left. He spent the rest of his days under the care of the congregation, greeting guests and writing letters to Christians around the world.

He, like the apostle Paul, indwelt a prison of misfortune. And he, like Paul, turned his cell into a commissary of hope. It's not easy to find joy in jail. Not easy to make the best of a derailed life. But God sends enough Paul and Joseph stories to convince us to give it a try.

Over a hundred years ago in England, the borough of West Stanley endured a great tragedy. A mine collapsed, trapping and killing many of the workers inside. The bishop of Durham, Dr. Handley Moule, was asked to bring a word of comfort to the mourners. Standing at the mouth of the mine, he said, "It is very difficult for us to understand why God should let such an awful disaster happen, but we know Him and we trust Him, and all will be right. I have at home," he continued, "an old bookmark given to me by my mother. It is worked in silk, and, when I examine the wrong side of it, I see nothing but a tangle of threads, crossed and re-crossed. It looks like a big mistake. One would think that someone had done it who did not know what she was doing. But when I turn it over and look at the right side, I see there, beautifully embroidered, the letters GOD IS LOVE.

"We are looking at this today," he counseled, "from the wrong side. Someday we shall see it from another standpoint, and shall understand."[3]

Indeed we shall. Until then, focus less on the tangled threads and more on the hand of the weaver. Learn a lesson from Vanderlei de Lima: don't let the bumps in the race keep you from the award ceremony at its end.

DAILY COMPASS

Where is your mind on your tough days? During the Friday of suffering, Jesus spoke thirteen times. Ten of those remarks were to or about God. Nearly 80 percent of his comments were heaven gilded. Jesus talked to or thought about God all day long.

The next time you fight through a season of Fridays, do the math. Does God consume 80 percent of your thoughts? He wants to. You can endure change by pondering his permanence. Survive rejection by meditating on his acceptance. When health fails you or problems disturb you, take a break from them! "Don't shuffle along, eyes to the ground . . . Look up, and be alert to what is going on around Christ—that's where the action is" (Colossians 3:2).

Follow the resolve of Paul: "We don't look at the troubles we can see now; rather, we fix our gaze on things that cannot be seen" (2 Corinthians 4:18 NLT). Christ can turn your toughest days into an Easter weekend.

7

<hr>

FUEL FOR DEPLETED DAYS

If you ever see a man walking on the side of the road carrying an empty gas can, remove your hat in respect. He's dying inside.

Women see the empty gas tank as an inconvenience. Men see it as the ultimate failure. Our first set of keys was handed to us with these words: "Make sure you buy some gas." From that moment on, the standard is set: take care of your machine.

All other measures of manhood pale in comparison. It matters not if you can transplant a heart or win the pentathlon. If you can't keep gas in your tank, you are of all men to be pitied. Such moments are etched in the memory of the male mind.

They linger in mine. In the days before the Lucado girls had driver's licenses, I served as their morning chauffeur. We were pulling into the school parking lot one day when the car hic-cuped. I looked down to see the gas needle resting on the wrong side of empty. Not wanting my daughters to see their father weep, I urged them to hurry on to class. It was one of my more noble gestures.

I then set about to solve the problem of the empty tank. I began by staring at the gauge, hoping it would move. Didn't work. Next I blamed my parents for potty training me too soon. Still no fuel. Denying the problem was my next approach. I put the car in gear and pressed the accelerator as if the tank were full. The car didn't budge.

Odd choices, you say? What do you do when you run out of gas? You don't exhaust your petroleum perhaps, but all of us run out of something. You need kindness, but the gauge is on empty. You need hope, but the needle is in the red. You want five gallons of solutions but can only muster a few drops. When you run out of steam before you run out of day, what do you do? Stare at the gauge? Blame your upbringing? Deny the problem?

No. Pity won't start the car. Complaints don't fuel an engine. Denial doesn't bump the needle. In the case of an empty tank, we've learned: get the car to a gas pump ASAP. In the case of the empty marriage, life, or heart, however, we tend to make the mis-take the disciples made.

They haven't run out of gas but out of food. Five thousand men and their families surround Jesus. They are getting hungry, and the disciples are getting antsy. "When it was late in the day, his followers came to him and said, 'No one lives in this place, and it is already very late'" (Mark 6:35 NCV).

His followers came to him. The five words imply an adjourned meeting. A committee had been formed, convened, and dismissed, all in the absence of Jesus. The disciples didn't consult their leader; they just described the problems and then told him what to do.

Problem number one: location. "No one lives in this place."

Problem number two: time. "It is already very late."

Problem number three: budget. In a parallel passage, Philip, the deacon in charge of finance, produces a just-printed pie chart. "Someone would have to work almost a year to buy enough bread for each person to have only a little piece" (John 6:7 NCV).

Do you detect an attitude behind those phrases? "No one lives in this place." (Who picked this venue?) "It's already very late." (Whoever preached forgot to watch the clock.) "We would all have to work a month." (Why didn't these people bring their own food?) The disciples' frustration borders on downright irreverence. Rather than *ask* Jesus what to do, they *tell* Jesus what to do. "Send the people away so they can go to the countryside and towns around here to buy themselves something to eat" (Mark 6:36 NCV). The disciples tell Jesus to tell the people to get lost.

Not one of their finer moments. Shouldn't they have known better? This is not the first problem they've seen Jesus face or fix. Rewind the tape and make a list of miracles they've witnessed. Water turned to wine, a boy healed in Capernaum, a boatload of fish caught at Galilee. They've seen Jesus raise a little girl from the dead, banish at least one demon, heal several paralytics and one mother-in-law. They've watched Jesus still a storm, resurrect a widow's son, and stop a twelve-year hemorrhage. So astounding were his healings that the following sentences appear in your Bible.

> Jesus healed many who had various diseases. He also drove out many demons. (Mark 1:34 NIV)

> Jesus went throughout Galilee . . . healing every disease and sickness among the people. . . . People brought to him all who were ill with various diseases, those suffering severe pain, the demon-possessed, those having seizures, and the paralyzed, and he healed them. (Matthew 4:23–24 NIV)

> The people all tried to touch him, because power was coming from him and healing them all. (Luke 6:19 NIV)

Veteran disciples have seen Jesus in action. The whole country has seen Jesus in action. He has earned a national reputation for doing the impossible. But do the disciples ask Jesus for his opinion? Does anyone in the committee meeting think about asking the miracle man what to do? Does John or Peter or James raise a hand and say, "Hey, I've got an idea. Let's go talk to the one who stilled the storm and raised the dead. Maybe he has a suggestion"?

Please note: the mistake of the disciples is not that they calculated the problem but that they calculated without Christ. In giving Jesus no chance, they gave their day no chance. They reserved a table for twelve at the Restaurant of the Rotten Day.

How unnecessary! If your father were Bill Gates and your computer broke, where would you turn? If Stradivari were your dad and your violin string snapped, to whom would you go? If your father is God and you have a problem on your hands, what do you do?

Scripture tells us what to do:

Is your problem too large? "God . . . is able . . . to accomplish infinitely more than we might ask or think" (Ephesians 3:20 NLT).

Is your need too great? "God is able to provide you with every blessing in abundance" (2 Corinthians 9:8 RSV).

Is your temptation too severe? "[God] is able to help us when we are being tested" (Hebrews 2:18 NLT).

Are your sins too numerous? "He is able, once and forever, to save those who come to God through him" (Hebrews 7:25 NLT).

Is your future too frightening? "God . . . is able to keep you from falling away and will bring you with great joy into his glorious presence without a single fault" (Jude 24 NLT).

Is your enemy too strong? "[God] is able even to subdue all things to Himself" (Philippians 3:21 NKJV).

Make these verses a part of your daily diet. God is able to accomplish, provide, help, save, keep, subdue . . . He is able to do what you can't. He already has a plan. Regarding the hungry crowd, "Jesus already knew what he planned to do" (John 6:6 NCV). God's not bewildered. Go to him.

My first thought when I ran out of fuel was *How can I get this car to a gas pump?* Your first thought when you have a problem should be *How can I get this problem to Jesus?*

Let's get practical. You and your spouse are about to battle it out again. The thunderstorm looms on the horizon. The temperature is dropping, and lightning bolts are flashing. Both of you need patience, but both tanks are empty. What if one of you calls, "Time-out"? What if one of you says, "Let's talk to Jesus before we talk to each other. In fact, let's talk to Jesus until we can talk to each other"? Couldn't hurt. After all, he broke down the walls of Jericho. Perhaps he could do the same for yours.

Another example: your coworker fouls up again and loses another client. You need ten buckets of patience yet have only a few drops. Rather than rush in and burn up what little patience you have, go first to Christ. Confess your weakness, and ask for help. Who knows, he might take your few drops and multiply them into a few gallons.

That's what he did for a young boy. Look how the story ends:

Andrew . . . said, "There's a little boy here who has five barley loaves and two fish. But that's a drop in the bucket for a crowd like this. . . ."

Then Jesus took the bread and, having given thanks, gave it to those who were seated. He did the same with the fish. All ate as much as they wanted.

When the people had eaten their fill, he said to his disciples, "Gather the leftovers so nothing is wasted." They went to work and filled twelve large baskets with leftovers from the five barley loaves.

The people realized that God was at work among them. (John 6:8–14)

The boy surfaces as the hero of the story. All he does is give his lunch to Jesus. He leaves the problem in the hands of the one with the oversight to do something about it.

It might surprise you to know that this boy, though silent in Scripture, was very verbal in life. Indeed, he was the first-century version of a rapper. In my extensive archaeological research, I uncovered this rap song written by the boy with the loaves and fishes. To feel its full impact, don some baggy shorts, turn your baseball cap sideways, and do your best gangsta sway.

Give It Up

by 5 Loaves

I had my loaves and had my fishes
Ready to eat, would be delicious,
But then the master took a look my way
And I knew why I was there that day, to
Give it up . . .
Give it up . . .

You got some struggles, got some fears?
Then listen to me, give me your ears.
Got a question, don't know where to ask it?
Do with it what I did with my basket—
Give it up . . .
Give it up . . .

Jesus got strength you know nothin' of.
His heart for you overflows with love.
He fed five thousand with scraps to spare.
He can meet your needs, take away your cares.
Give it up . . .
Give it up . . .

However you say it or sing it, the point is the same: God is able to do what you can't. So give your problem to Jesus. Don't make the mistake of the disciples. They analyzed, organized, evaluated, and calculated—all without Jesus. The result? They became anxious and bossy.

Go first to Christ. You're going to run out of gas. We all do. Next time the needle sits on the wrong side of empty, remember: the one who fed the crowds is a prayer away.

DAILY COMPASS

The next time life's problems overwhelm you, remember this advice from Peter: "Throw the whole weight of your anxieties upon him, for you are his personal concern" (1 Peter 5:7 PHILLIPS).

"Unload all your worries on to him, since he is looking after you" (JB).

"Cast all your anxieties on him, for he cares about you" (RSV).

Translate the message however you wish, the point is the same:

God's solution is a prayer away!

8

---◇◇◇---

FAITH FOR
FEAR-FILLED DAYS

Do you think he can?"

"Do you think he cares?"

"Do you think he'll come?"

The questions emerge from the mother's heart. Fear drapes her words and shadows her face.

Her husband stops at the door of their house and looks back into her tired, frightened eyes, then over her shoulder at the figure of his sick daughter lying on the pallet. The girl shivers from the fever. The mother shakes from the fear. The father shrugs in desperation and answers, "I don't know what he'll do, but I don't know what else to do."

The crowd outside the house parts to let the father pass. They would on any day. He is the city leader. But they do this day because his daughter is dying.

"Bless you, Jairus," one offers. But Jairus doesn't stop. He hears only the questions of his wife.

"Do you think he can?"

"Do you think he cares?"

"Do you think he'll come?"

Jairus steps quickly down the path through the fishing village of Capernaum. The size of the following crowd increases with every person he passes. They know where Jairus goes. They know whom he seeks. Jairus goes to the shore to seek Jesus. As they near the water's edge, they spot the Teacher, encircled by a multitude. A citizen steps ahead to clear a trail, announcing the presence of the synagogue ruler. Villagers comply. The Red Sea of humanity parts, leaving a people-walled path. Jairus wastes no seconds. "When he saw Jesus, he fell to his knees, beside himself as he begged, 'My dear daughter is at death's door. Come and lay hands on her so she will get well and live.' Jesus went with him, the whole crowd tagging along, pushing and jostling him" (Mark 5:22–24).

Jesus' instant willingness moistens the eyes of Jairus. For the first time in a long time, a sun ray lands on the father's soul. He all but runs as he leads Jesus back to the path toward home. Jairus dares to believe he is moments from a miracle.

Jesus *can* help.

Jesus *does* care.

Jesus *is* coming.

People scatter out of the way and step in behind. Servants rush ahead to inform Jairus's wife. But then, just as suddenly as Jesus started, Jesus stops. Jairus, unaware, takes a dozen more steps before he realizes he's walking alone. The people stopped when Jesus did. And everyone is trying to make sense of Jesus' question: "Who touched my clothes?" (5:30 NIV). The sentence triggers a rush of activity. Heads turn toward each other; disciples respond to Christ. Someone moves back so someone else can come forward.

Jairus can't see who. And, quite frankly, he doesn't care who. Precious seconds are passing. His precious daughter is passing. Moments ago he grand-marshaled the Hope Parade. Now he stands on the outside looking in and feels his fragile faith unravel. He looks toward his house and back at Christ and wonders afresh:

I wonder if he can.

I wonder if he cares.

I wonder if he'll come.

We know the questions of Jairus, because we've faced the fear of Jairus. His Capernaum is our hospital, courthouse, or lonely highway. His dying daughter is our dying marriage, career, future, or friend. Jairus is not the last to ask Jesus for a miracle.

We've done the same. With belief weighing a feather more than unbelief, we've fallen at Jesus' feet and begged. He replies with hope. His answer couriers fresh light. The cloud parts. The sun shines . . . for a time.

But halfway to the miracle, Jesus stops. The illness returns, the heart hardens, the factory closes, the check bounces, the criticism resumes, and we find ourselves with Jairus, on the outside looking in, feeling like a low item on God's to-do list, wondering if Jesus remembers. Wondering if he can, cares, or comes.

Jairus feels a touch on his shoulder. He turns to look into the pale face of a sad servant, who tells him, "Your daughter is dead. Do not trouble the Teacher" (Luke 8:49 NKJV).

It's fallen to me on a few occasions to fulfill the task of this servant. To bear death tidings. I've informed a father of the death of his teenage son, my siblings of the death of our dad, more than one child of the death of a parent.

Each announcement is met with silence. Wailing or fainting may soon follow, but the first response is a shock-soaked silence. As if no heart can receive the words and no words can express the heart. No one knows what to say to death.

Was it into such a silence that Jesus urged, "Don't be afraid; just believe" (Mark 5:36 NIV)?

Believe? Jairus might have thought. *Believe what? Believe how? Believe who? My daughter is dead. My wife is distraught. And you, Jesus, well, you are late. Had you come when I asked, followed when I led . . . Why did you let my little girl die?*

Jairus had no way of knowing the answer. But we do. Why did Jesus let the girl die? So that two thousand years' worth of strugglers would hear Jesus' response to human tragedy. To all who have stood where Jairus stood and asked what Jairus asked, Jesus says, "Don't be afraid; just believe."

Believe that he can. Believe that he is able to help.

Note how the story takes a sudden turn. Until this point Jesus has followed the lead of Jairus; now he takes control. He commandeers the scene. He trims his team down to fighting size: "And He permitted no one to follow Him except Peter, James, and John the brother of James" (5:37 NKJV).

Jesus tells the mourners to clam up. "When He came in, He said to them, 'Why make this commotion and weep? The child is not dead, but sleeping'" (5:39 NKJV).

When they mock him, "He . . . put them all outside" (5:40 NKJV). The English translation softens the action. The Greek uses a bare-knuckled verb; *ekballo* means to cast out or throw out. Jesus, the temple cleanser and demon caster, rolls up his sleeves. He's the sheriff in the rowdy saloon placing one hand on shirt collar and the other on trouser belt and tossing the troublemaking doubt-stirrers into the street.

He then turns his attention to the body of the girl. He bears the confidence of Einstein adding two plus two, Beethoven playing "Chopsticks," Ben Hogan approaching a one-inch putt. Can Jesus call the dead to life? Of course he can.

But does he care? Might he be mighty *and* tender? Have muscle *and* mercy? Does the plight of a twelve-year-old girl in Podunkville appear on the radar screen of heaven?

An earlier moment in the story reveals the answer. It's subtle. You might have missed it. "As soon as Jesus heard the word that was spoken, He said to the ruler of the synagogue, 'Do not be afraid; only believe'" (5:36 NKJV).

Jesus heard the servant's words. No one had to tell him about the girl's death. Though separated from Jairus, occupied with the case of the woman, encircled by pressing villagers, Jesus never took his ear off the girl's father. Jesus was listening the entire time. He heard. He cared. He cared enough to speak to Jairus's fear, to come to Jairus's home.

> He took the father and the mother of the child, and those who were with Him, and entered where the child was lying. Then He took the child by the hand, and said to her, "Talitha, cumi," which is translated, "Little girl, I say to you, arise." Immediately the girl arose and walked. (5:40–42 NKJV)

A pronouncement from the path would have worked. A declaration from afar would have awakened the girl's heart. But Jesus wanted to do more than raise the dead. He wanted to show that he not only can and cares but that he comes.

Into the houses of Jairuses. Into the world of his children. He comes to those as small as Mary's baby and as poor as a carpenter's boy. He comes to those as young as a Nazarene teenager and as forgotten as an unnoticed kid in an obscure village. He comes to those as busy as the oldest son of a large family, to those as stressed as the leader of restless disciples, to those as tired as one with no pillow for his head.

He comes to all. He speaks to all. He spoke to me this week. The book you are reading came back from my editors with a hemorrhage of red ink. A tattoo parlor gives fewer mark ups than they did. For two days I dreaded the mountain of work ahead of me. I seriously considered shelving the project. The irony of my rotten attitude struck me: writing a book about good days was taking the fun out of mine.

Denalyn suggested I take a break and accompany her to the grocery store. (You're in bad shape when the idea of pushing a grocery cart through the meat department sounds nice.) A member of our congregation spotted me.

After a few niceties he asked, "Remember those lessons you taught on giving every day a chance?"

More than you can imagine. "I do."

"They really helped me."

"Glad to know that."

"No, Max," he said, giving me an "I'm serious" tone. "I mean they really helped."

So much for shelving the manuscript. Sometimes we just need a word, don't we? And God still gives it. To the overwhelmed. To the downcast. To Jairus. To us. He still urges:

"Don't be afraid; just believe."

Believe that he can, believe that he cares, believe that he comes. Oh how we need to believe. Fear pillages so much peace from our days.

When ancient sailors sketched maps of the oceans, they disclosed their fears. On the vast unexplored waters, cartographers wrote words such as these:

"Here be dragons."

"Here be demons."

"Here be sirens."

Were a map drawn of your world, would we read such phrases? Over the unknown waters of adulthood "Here be dragons." Near the sea of the empty nest "Here be demons." Next to the farthermost latitudes of death and eternity, do we read "Here be sirens"?

If so, take heart from the example of Sir John Franklin. He was a master mariner in the days of King Henry V. Distant waters were a mystery to him, just as they were to other navigators. Unlike his colleagues, however, Sir John Franklin was a man of faith. The maps that passed through his possession bore the imprimatur of trust. On them he had crossed out the phrases "Here be dragons," "Here be demons," "Here be sirens." In their place he wrote the phrase "Here is God."[1]

Mark it down. You will never go where God is not. You may be transferred, enlisted, commissioned, reassigned, or hospitalized, but—brand this truth on your heart—you can never go where God is not. "I am with you always," Jesus promised (Matthew 28:20 NKJV).

Don't be afraid; just believe.

The presence of fear does not mean you have no faith. Fear visits everyone. Even Christ was afraid (Mark 14:33). But make your fear a visitor and not a resident. Hasn't fear taken enough? Enough smiles? Chuckles? Restful nights, exuberant days? Meet your fears with faith.

Do what my father urged my brother and me to do. Summertime for the Lucado family always involved a trip from West Texas to the Rocky Mountains. (Think Purgatory to Paradise.) My dad loved to fish for trout on the edge of the white-water rivers. Yet he knew that the currents were dangerous and his sons could be careless. Upon arrival we'd scout out the safe places to cross the river. He'd walk us down the bank until we found a line of stable rocks. He was even known to add one or two to compensate for our short strides.

As we watched, he'd test the stones, knowing if they held him, they'd hold us. Once on the other side, he'd signal for us to follow.

"Don't be afraid," he could have said. "Trust me."

We children never needed coaxing. But we adults often do. Does a river of fear run between you and Jesus? Cross over to him. Had Jairus waved Jesus away, death would have taken his hope. If you wave Jesus away, joy will die, laughter will perish, and tomorrow will be buried in today's grave of dread.

Don't make that mistake. Give the day a chance. Believe he can. Believe he cares. Believe he comes. Don't be afraid. Just believe.

DAILY COMPASS

Brighten your day by envisioning God running toward you.

When his patriarchs trusted, God blessed. When Peter preached or Paul wrote or Thomas believed, God smiled. But he never ran.

That verb was reserved for the story of the prodigal son. "But when he was still a great way off, his father saw him and had compassion, and ran and fell on his neck and kissed him" (Luke 15:20 NKJV).

God runs when he sees the son coming home from the pig trough. When the addict steps out of the alley. When the teen walks away from the party. When the ladder-climbing executive pushes back from the desk, the spiritist turns from idols, the materialist from stuff, the atheist from disbelief, and the elitist from self-promotion . . .

When prodigals trudge up the path, God can't sit still. Heaven's throne room echoes with the sound of slapping sandals and pounding feet, and angels watch in silence as God embraces his child.

You turn toward God, and he runs toward you.

SECTION 3

ACCEPT HIS DIRECTION

---◇---

Posted outside the choir rehearsal room was this flyer:

High School Musical:
Oklahoma!
Tryouts next Thursday and Friday

My opportunity at last! If Buddy Holly and Roy Orbison could make the leap from West Texas to the big stage, why couldn't I? I was a high school sophomore, brimming with untapped and undiscovered talent. Besides, I already had the boots, hat, and accent. Why not give it a go?

My audition was stellar, until I opened my mouth to sing. The music director covered his ears and placed his head between his knees. Outside the window, a dog began to howl. On the wall, paint began to curl. Still, the director said he might have a spot for me. He asked if I had theater experience. I told him I went to the movies about once a month. That was enough for him. He gave me a script and the page number on which I would find my part. That's right, page number. Not page *numbers*. Page *number*.

My part fit on one page. Check that. One paragraph on one page. More accurately, one line in one paragraph on one page.

Decades later I still remember both words. Having knelt over the body of a just-shot cowboy, I was to lift my head and cry in desperation, "He's daid!" Not "He's dead," but "He's d-a-i-d, daid!"

Others might resent such a diminutive role. Not me. Were my words not essential? Someone has to announce a stage death. I poured my soul into that line. Why, had you looked closely enough, you might have spotted the tiny tear forming in the corner of my eye.

Rodgers and Hammerstein would have been proud. But, of course, they never knew. When they wrote their story, they weren't thinking of me. But when God wrote his, he was thinking of us all.

What's your part? Don't think for a moment that you don't have one. God "shaped each person in turn" (Psalm 33:15). "Each of us is an original" (Galatians 5:26). He cast you in his play, wrote you into his story. No assignment too small. No lines too brief. He has a definite direction for your life. Fulfill it and enjoy fulfillment. Play the part God prepared for you, and get ready for some great days.

9

---◇◆◇---

CALLING FOR
PURPOSELESS DAYS

Simon grumbles under his breath. His patience is as scarce as space on the Jerusalem streets. He'd hoped for a peaceful Passover. The city is anything but quiet. Simon prefers his open fields. And now, to top it off, the Roman guards are clearing the path for some who-knows-which dignitary who'll march his soldiers and strut his stallion past the people.

"There he is!"

Simon's head and dozens of others turn. In an instant they know. This is no dignitary.

"It's a crucifixion," he hears someone whisper. Four soldiers. One criminal. Four spears. One cross. The inside corner of the cross saddles the convict's shoulders. Its base drags in the dirt. Its top teeters in the air. The condemned man steadies the cross the best he can but stumbles beneath its weight. He pushes himself to his feet and lurches forward before falling again. Simon can't see the man's face, only a head wreathed with thorny branches.

A sour-faced centurion grows more agitated with each diminishing step. He curses the criminal and the crowd.

"Hurry up!"

"Little hope of that," Simon says to himself.

The cross-bearer stops in front of Simon and heaves for air. Simon winces at what he sees. The beam rubbing against an already-raw back. Rivulets of crimson streaking the man's face. His mouth hangs open, both out of pain and out of breath.

"His name is Jesus," someone speaks softly.

"Move on!" commands the executioner.

But Jesus can't. His body leans and feet try, but he can't move. The beam begins to sway. Jesus tries to steady it, but can't. Like a just-cut tree, the cross begins to topple toward the crowd. Everyone steps back, except the farmer. Simon instinctively extends his strong hands and catches the cross.

Jesus falls face-first in the dirt and stays there. Simon pushes the cross back on its side. The centurion looks at the exhausted Christ and the bulky bystander and needs only an instant to make the decision. He presses the flat of his spear on Simon's shoulder.

"You! Take the cross!"

Simon dares to object. "Sir, I don't even know the man!"

"I don't care. Take up the cross."

Simon growls, steps out of the crowd onto the street, and

balances the timber against his shoulder, out of anonymity into history, and becomes the first in a line of millions who will take up the cross and follow Christ. "A man named Simon from Cyrene, the father of Alexander and Rufus, was coming from the fields to the city. The soldiers forced Simon to carry the cross for Jesus" (Mark 15:21 NCV). "They forced him to carry Jesus' cross and to walk behind him" (Luke 23:26 NCV).

Such sketchy details: a foreigner from Cyrene, coming in from the fields, forced to carry the cross. Had Simon ever heard of Christ? What was he doing in Jerusalem? Why the reference to his two sons? We don't know. All we know for certain is this:

He shouldered the cross of Christ. He did literally what God calls us to do figuratively: take up the cross and follow Jesus. "If any of you want to be my followers, you must forget about yourself. You must take up your cross each day and follow me" (Luke 9:23 CEV).

The phrase "take up your cross" has not fared well through the generations. Ask for a definition, and you'll hear answers like, "My cross is my mother-in-law, my job, my bad marriage, my cranky boss, or the dull preacher." The cross, we assume, is any besetting affliction or personal hassle. My thesaurus agrees. It lists the following synonyms for *cross*: *frustration, trying situation, snag, hitch,* and *drawback.* To take up the cross is to put up with a personal challenge. God, we think, passes out crosses the way a warden hands out shovels to the chain gang. No one wants one. Each one gets one. Everybody has a cross to bear, and we might as well get used to it.

But really. Is Jesus reducing the cross to hassles and

headaches? Calling us to quit complaining about the fly in the ointment or the pain in the neck? The cross means so much more. It is God's tool of redemption, instrument of salvation— proof of his love for people. To take up the cross, then, is to take up Christ's burden for the people of the world.

Though our crosses are similar, none are identical. "If any of you want to be my followers, you must forget about yourself. You must take up *your cross* each day and follow me" (Luke 9:23 CEV, emphasis mine).

We each have our own cross to carry—our individual calling. Yours awaits you like a snug-fitting shirt. We all know the discomfort of a poor-fitting one. Being the baby in my family, I inherited my share of hand-me-downs from my brother. They covered my flesh, but failed to fit my body. Tight cloth pinched my shoulders, and the collar draped on my neck. It was a fine day when Mom decided to buy me shirts that fit.

It's an even sweeter day when you discover your God-designed task. It fits. It matches your passions and enlists your gifts and talents. Want to blow the cloud cover off your gray day? Accept God's direction.

John Bentley did. He carries a cross for Chinese orphans. This Christian lawyer has hung his shingle in Beijing, where he and his wife oversee an orphanage for abandoned babies. Some years ago a mother deposited a newborn, dressed in burial clothes, in a nearby field. No note, no explanation, just the Chinese equivalent of $1.25: the price of a burial. The mother had abandoned her child. One examination revealed why. The child was severely burned from head to toe.

The Bentleys could not let the child die. They not only nursed the boy back to health, but they adopted him as their son. They carry the cross of Christ for the children of China.

Michael Landon Jr. carries one for the film industry. He's uniquely qualified to do so. The son of a television legend, he grew up in the movie business. When Christ claimed his nineteen-year-old heart, he set out to influence the world of entertainment. He pours daily energy and credibility into one task: creating redemptive films. Few have the training or the experience to do what he does. But since Michael has both, he daily shoulders the cross of Christ for Hollywood.

Shawn and Xochitl Hughes carry the cross for San Antonio's central city. As others were moving out, they moved in. They chose a simple neighborhood over an extravagant one, a small house over a large one. They love the hearts in the heart of our city. Call it a passion, a burden . . . call it a cross. They've taken up a cross.

"The Lord has assigned to each his task" (1 Corinthians 3:5 NIV). What is yours? What is your unique call, assignment, mission?

A trio of questions might help.

In what directions has God taken you? Tally up the experiences unique to you. "Don't act thoughtlessly, but try to find out and do whatever the Lord wants you to" (Ephesians 5:17 TLB). In what culture were you raised? To what lifestyles have you been exposed? Your past is a signpost to your future. Ask Moses. His Egyptian childhood experiences prepared him to stand before Pharaoh. David grew up herding sheep. Not bad training for one called to pastor a nation. Paul's pedigree as a Roman citizen likely extended his life and his ministry. Your past is no accident.

What about your burdens? *What needs has God revealed to you?* What makes your heart race and blood pump? Not everyone weeps when you do. Not everyone hurts like you do. Heed the hurts of your heart. We each "run with patience the particular race that God has set before us" (Hebrews 12:1 TLB). Do you know your event?

What abilities has God given to you? "Christ has given each of us special abilities" (Ephesians 4:7 TLB). What comes easy to you? Some of you can manage large numbers. Others manage large orders. You excel at something and do so with comparatively little effort. Daniel Sharp grew up at the church where I serve. As part of his college education, he moved to Moscow to study calculus, electricity, magnetism, and poetry—in Russian. He found the courses so fun that he e-mailed his parents, "Can't anyone do this?" I don't think so. But the fact that Daniel can says something about his unique call in life.[1]

Something comes easy for you as well. Identify it! "Make a careful exploration of who you are" (Galatians 6:4).

Direction. Need. Ability. Your spiritual *DNA*. You at your best. You and your cross.

While none of us is called to carry the sin of the world (Jesus did that), all of us can carry a burden for the world.

By the way, this is a wonderful burden. Jesus said, "The load I give you to carry is light" (Matthew 11:30 NCV). The cross is a good weight, a sweet debt. Test this truth. Visit people in the hospital. See if you don't leave happier than when you entered.

Teach a class for kids. See if you don't learn more than they do. Dedicate a Saturday to helping the homeless. You'll discover this mystery: as you help others face their days, you put life into your own. And life is exactly what many people need. This amazing article appeared in a British newspaper.

> Bosses of a publishing firm are trying to work out why no one noticed that one of their employees had been sitting dead at his desk for five days before anyone asked if he was feeling OK.
>
> George Turklebaum, 51, who had been employed as a proofreader at a New York firm for 30 years, had a heart attack in the open-plan office he shared with 23 other workers.
>
> He quietly passed away on Monday but nobody noticed until Saturday morning when an office cleaner asked why he was still working during the weekend.[2]

The account prompts two quick questions. Could this really happen? Could a dead person pass for a living one? And second, could this happen to us? Could we be so void of life, vacated of emotion, excavated of excitement that we could die and no one know it?

Check your vital signs. Something stirs you. Some call brings energy to your voice, conviction to your face, and direction to your step. Isolate and embrace it. Nothing gives a day a greater chance than a good wallop of passion.

DAILY COMPASS

Ask God to inject his passion in your day.

Pray for every person you pass. Don't grumble in traffic jams or complain in crowded elevators. These are prayer moments. Intercede for each person you see, "praying always with all prayer" (Ephesians 6:18 NKJV). Imitate Epaphras, who Paul said was "always laboring fervently for you in prayers" (Colossians 4:12 NKJV). He labored, strove, worked in prayers. I'm envisioning a strained face, tearful cheeks, clenched hands.

Stir spiritual dialogue. At the right time, with the right heart, ask your friends and family, "What do you think happens after we die?" "What is your view of God?" Jesus asked such questions: "Who do you say I am?" (Mark 8:29 NIV). Let's ask them too.

Love because God loves. People can be tough to love. Love them anyway. "He who loves God must love his brother also" (1 John 4:21 NKJV).

10

◦◇◦

SERVICE FOR
FORK-IN-THE-ROAD DAYS

Dan Mazur considered himself lucky. Most other people would have considered him crazy. He stood within a two-hour hike of the summit of Mount Everest, a thousand feet from realizing a lifelong dream.

Every year the fittest adventurers on earth set their sights on the twenty-nine-thousand–foot peak. Every year some die in the effort. The top of Everest isn't known for its hospitality. Climbers call the realm above twenty-six thousand feet "the death zone."

Temperatures hover below zero. Sudden blizzards stir blinding snow. The atmosphere is oxygen starved. Corpses dot the mountaintop. A British climber had died ten days prior to Mazur's attempt. Forty climbers who could have helped chose not to do so. They passed him on the way to the summit.

Everest can be cruel.

Still, Mazur felt lucky. He and two colleagues were within eyesight of the top. Years of planning. Six weeks of climbing, and now at 7:30 a.m., May 25, 2006, the air was still, morning sun brilliant, energy and hopes high.

That's when a flash of color caught Mazur's eye: a bit of yellow fabric on the ridgetop. He first thought it was a tent. He soon saw it was a person, a man precariously perched on an eight-thousand-foot razor-edge rock. His gloves were off, jacket unzipped, hands exposed, chest bare. Oxygen deprivation can swell the brain and stir hallucinations. Mazur knew this man had no idea where he was, so he walked toward him and called out.

"Can you tell me your name?"

"Yes," the man answered, sounding pleased. "I can. My name is Lincoln Hall."

Mazur was shocked. He recognized this name. Twelve hours earlier he'd heard the news on the radio: "Lincoln Hall is dead on the mountain. His team has left his body on the slope."

And yet, after spending the night in twenty-below chill and oxygen-stingy air, Lincoln Hall was still alive. Mazur was face-to-face with a miracle.

He was also face-to-face with a choice. A rescue attempt had profound risks. The descent was already treacherous, even more so with the dead weight of a dying man. Besides, how long would Hall survive? No one knew. The three climbers might sacrifice their Everest for naught. They had to choose: abandon their dream or abandon Lincoln Hall.

They chose to abandon their dream. The three turned their backs on the peak and inched their way down the mountain.[1]

Their decision to save Hall's life stirs a great question. Would we do the same? Surrender ambition to save someone else? Set aside our dreams to rescue another climber? Turn our backs on our personal mountaintops so someone else might live?

We make such fork-in-the-road decisions daily. Not on Everest with adventurers, but in homes with spouses and children, at work with colleagues, in schools with friends, in churches with fellow believers. We regularly face subtle yet significant decisions, all of which fall under the category of who comes first: do they or do I?

When the parent chooses the best school for the children over a career-advancing transfer.

When the student eats lunch with the neglected kids rather than the cool ones.

When the grown daughter spends her days off with her aging mother at the dementia unit.

When you turn away from personal dreams for the sake of others, you are, in Christ's words, denying yourself. "If any of you wants to be my follower, you must turn from your selfish ways, take up your cross, and follow me" (Matthew 16:24 NLT).

Behold the most surprising ingredient of a great day: self-denial.

Don't we assume just the opposite? Great days emerge from the soil of self-indulgence, self-expression, and self-celebration.

So pamper yourself, indulge yourself, promote yourself. But deny yourself? When was the last time you read this ad copy: "Go ahead. Deny yourself and have the time of your life!"?

Jesus could have written the words. He often goes counter-cultural, calling us down rather than up, telling us to zig when society says to zag.

In his economy,

- the least are the greatest (Luke 9:48);
- the last will be first (Mark 9:35);
- the chosen seats are the forgotten seats
  (Luke 14:8–9).

He tells us to

- honor others above ourselves (Romans 12:10);
- consider others better than ourselves (Philippians
  2:3);
- turn the other cheek, give away our coats, and walk
  the second mile (Matthew 5:39–41).

That last instruction surely struck a raw nerve in the Jewish psyche. "Whoever compels you to go one mile, go with him two" (Matthew 5:41 NKJV). Jesus' fellow citizens lived under foreign rule. Roman soldiers imposed high taxes and oppressive laws. This sad state of affairs had existed ever since the Babylonians had destroyed the temple in 586 BC and carried the Judeans into captivity. Though some had returned from geographical exile, the theological and political exile lingered. First-century Jews were sloshing through a centuries-old morass: oppressed by pagans, looking for the Messiah to deliver them.

Some responded by selling out, working the system to their own advantage. Others got out. The writers of the Dead Sea Scrolls at Qumran chose to separate themselves from the wicked world. Still others decided to fight back. The Zealot option was clear: say your prayers, sharpen your sword, and fight a holy war.

Three options: sell out, get out, or fight back.

Jesus introduced a fourth. Serve. Serve the ones who hate you; forgive the ones who hurt you. Take the lowest place, not the highest; seek to serve, not to be served. Retaliate, not in kind but in kindness. He created what we might deem the Society of the Second Mile.

Roman soldiers could legally coerce Jewish citizens into carrying their load for one mile.[2] With nothing more than a command, they could requisition a farmer out of his field or a merchant out of his shop.

In such a case, Jesus said, "Give more than requested." Go two. At the end of one mile, keep going. Surprise the sandals off the soldier by saying, "I haven't done enough for you. I'm going a second mile." Do more than demanded. And do so with joy and grace!

The Society of the Second Mile still exists. Its members surrender Everest-level ambitions so they can help weary climbers find safety.

We have a second-mile servant in our church. By profession he is an architect. By passion, a servant. He arrives an hour or so prior to each worship service and makes his rounds through the men's restrooms. He wipes the sinks, cleans the mirrors, checks the toilets, and picks up paper off the floor. No one asked him to do the work; very few people are aware he does the work. He tells no one and requests nothing in return. He belongs to the Society of the Second Mile.

Another second-miler serves in our children's ministry. She creates crafts and take-home gifts for four-year-olds. Completing the craft is not enough, however. She has to give it a second-mile touch. When a class followed the theme "Walking in the Steps of Jesus," she made cookies in the shape of a foot and, in second-mile fashion, painted a toenail on each cookie. Who does that?

Second-milers do. They clean bathrooms, decorate cookies, and build playrooms in their houses. At least Bob and Elsie did. They built an indoor pool, bought a Ping-Pong table and foosball game. They created a kid's paradise.

Not unusual, you say? Oh, I forgot to mention their age. They did this in their seventies. They did this because they loved the lonely youth of downtown Miami. Bob didn't swim. Elsie didn't play Ping-Pong. But the kids of immigrant Cubans did. And Bob could be seen each week driving his Cadillac through Little Havana, picking up the teens other people forgot.

The Society of the Second Mile. Let me tell you how to spot its members. They don't wear badges or uniforms; they wear smiles. They have discovered the secret. The joy is found in the extra effort. The sweetest satisfaction lies not in climbing your own Everest but in helping other climbers.

Second-milers read Jesus' statement that it is better to give than receive (Acts 20:35) and nod their heads. When they hear the instruction "If your first concern is to look after yourself, you'll never find yourself" (Matthew 10:39), they understand. They've discovered this truth: "Self-help is no help at all. Self-sacrifice is the way, my way, to finding yourself, your true self" (Luke 9:24).

The real reward rests at the base of the second-mile post.

Think of it this way. Imagine yourself as a twelve-year-old facing a sink of dirty dishes. You don't want to wash them. You'd rather play with your friends or watch television. But your mom has made it clear: clean the dishes.

You groan, moan, and wonder how you might place yourself for adoption. Then, from who knows where, a wacky idea strikes you. What if you surprise your mom by cleaning, not just the dishes, but the entire kitchen? You begin to smile. "I'll sweep the floor and wipe down the cabinets. Maybe reorganize the refrigerator!" And from some unknown source comes a shot of energy, a surge of productivity. A dull task becomes an adventure. Why? Liberation! You've passed from slave to volunteer.

This is the joy of the second mile.

Have you found it? Your day moves with the speed of an ice floe and the excitement of a quilting tournament. You do what is required—math problems and one chapter in literature—but no more. You are reliable, dependable, and quite likely bored. You dream of Fridays, holidays, a different family or a different job, when maybe all you need is a different attitude. Give your day a chance.

Daily do a deed for which you cannot be repaid.

In the final days of Jesus' life, he shared a meal with his friends Lazarus, Martha, and Mary. Within the week he would feel the sting of the Roman whip, the point of the thorny crown, and the iron of the executioner's nail. But on this evening, he felt the love of three friends.

For Mary, however, giving the dinner was not enough. "Mary came in with a jar of very expensive aromatic oils, anointed and massaged Jesus' feet, and then wiped them with her hair. The fragrance of the oils filled the house" (John 12:3).

One-milers among the group, like Judas, criticized the deed as wasteful. Not Jesus. He received the gesture as an extravagant demonstration of love, a friend surrendering her most treasured gift. As Jesus hung on the cross, we wonder, *Did he detect the fragrance on his skin?*

Follow Mary's example.

There is an elderly man in your community who just lost his wife. An hour of your time would mean the world to him.

Some kids in your city have no dad. No father takes them to movies or baseball games. Maybe you can. They can't pay you back. They can't even afford the popcorn or sodas. But they'll smile like a cantaloupe slice at your kindness.

Or how about this one? Down the hall from your bedroom is a person who shares your last name. Shock that person with kindness. Something outlandish. Your homework done with no complaints. Coffee served before he awakens. A love letter written to her for no special reason. Alabaster poured, just because.

Want to snatch a day from the manacles of boredom? Do

overgenerous deeds, acts beyond reimbursement. Kindness without compensation. Do a deed for which you cannot be repaid.

Here's another idea. *Get over yourself.*

Moses did. One of history's foremost leaders was "a very humble man, more humble than anyone else on the face of the earth" (Numbers 12:3 NIV).

Mary did. When Jesus called her womb his home, she did not boast; she simply confessed: "I'm the Lord's maid, ready to serve" (Luke 1:38).

John the Baptist did. Though a blood relative of God on earth, he made this choice: "This is the assigned moment for him to move into the center, while I slip off to the sidelines" (John 3:30).

Most of all, Jesus did. "Jesus . . . was given a position 'a little lower than the angels'" (Hebrews 2:9 NLT).

Jesus chose the servants' quarters. Can't we?

We're important but not essential, valuable but not indispensable. We have a part in the play, but we are not the main act. A song to sing, but we are not the featured voice.

God is.

He did well before our births; he'll do fine after our deaths. He started it all, sustains it all, and will bring it all to a glorious climax. In the meantime, we have this high privilege: to surrender personal Everests, discover the thrill of the doubled distance, do deeds for which we cannot be paid, seek problems that others avoid, deny ourselves, take up our crosses, and follow Christ.

Lincoln Hall survived the trip down Mount Everest. Thanks to Dan Mazur, he lived to be reunited with his wife and sons in

New Zealand. A television reporter asked Lincoln's wife what she thought of the rescuers, the men who surrendered their summit to save her husband's life. She tried to answer, but the words stuck in her throat. After several moments and with tear-filled eyes, she offered, "Well, there's one amazing human being. And the other men with him. The world needs more people like that."[3]

May we be numbered among them.

DAILY COMPASS

Teach us how short our lives really are so that we may be wise" (Psalm 90:12 NCV).

If today were your last day of life, how would you spend it? Facing death is bitter medicine, but most of us could use a spoonful. Most of us could benefit from a death reminder. You don't want one, and I can't say I enjoy giving one, but we need to know: we are one day closer to death than we were yesterday.

If today were your last, would you do what you're doing? Or would you love more, give more, forgive more? Then do so! Forgive and give as if it were your last opportunity. Love like there's no tomorrow, and if tomorrow comes, love again.

CONCLUSION

—◇◇◇—

THE BLADE OF
UNCOMMON COLOR

*Don't shuffle along, eyes to the ground. . . . Look up, and
be alert to what is going on around Christ. . . . See things
from his perspective.*

—COLOSSIANS 3:2

Dirt carpeted the floor. Rats scurried beneath the grated vent.
Roaches roamed the walls and crawled over sleeping prisoners.
The only source of light peeked through three holes near the
fifteen-foot ceiling. The cell offered no bunk, no chair, no table,
and no way out for American General Robbie Risner. For seven
and one-half years, North Vietnamese soldiers held him and
dozens of other soldiers in the Zoo, a POW camp in Hanoi.

Misery came standard issue. Solitary confinement, starvation,
torture, and beatings were routine. Interrogators twisted broken

legs, sliced skin with bayonets, crammed sticks up nostrils and paper in mouths. Screams echoed throughout the camp, chilling the blood of other prisoners.

Listen to Risner's description: "Everything was sad and dismal. It was almost the essence of despair. If you could have squeezed the feeling out of the word *despair*, it would have come out gray, dull, and lead-colored, dingy and dirty."[1]

How do you survive seven and one-half years in such a hole? Cut off from family. No news from the United States. What do you do? Here is what Risner did. He stared at a blade of grass. Several days into his incarceration he wrestled the grate off a floor vent, stretched out on his belly, lowered his head into the opening, and peered through a pencil-sized hole in the brick and mortar at a singular blade of grass. Aside from this stem, his world had no color. So he began his days with head in vent, heart in prayer, staring at the green blade of grass. He called it a "blood transfusion for the soul."[2]

You don't have to go to Hanoi to face a "gray, dull, and lead-colored, dingy and dirty" existence. Do you know the tint of a colorless world? If so, do what Risner did. Go on a search. Crowbar the grate from your cell, and stick your head out. Fix your eyes on a color outside your cell.

What you see defines who you are. "Your eyes are windows into your body. If you open your eyes wide in wonder and belief, your body fills up with light. If you live squinty-eyed in greed and distrust, your body is a dank cellar. If you pull the blinds on your windows, what a dark life you will have!" (Matthew 6:22–23).

Jesus is discussing not the eyes of your head but the eyes of your heart—your attitude, your outlook, your vision, not of things but of life. We, like General Risner, make daily decisions. Do we set our eyes on the gray harshness or search for the blade of a different color?

Jerry Rushford directs the Pepperdine Lectureship each year in Malibu, California. He masterfully coordinates a week of classes and speakers, hundreds of teachers and thousands of attendees. You'd be hard-pressed to find anything wrong with the event, but inevitably someone does. For that reason Jerry always closes the final session with this tongue-in-cheek phrase: "If you look hard enough, long enough, you'll find, I'm sure, something to complain about. But we hope you'll look at the good."

If you look hard enough and long enough, you'll find something to complain about.

Adam and Eve did. Doesn't the bite into the forbidden fruit reflect a feeling of discontent? Surrounded by all they needed, they set their eyes on the one thing they couldn't have. They found something to complain about.

The followers of Moses did. They could have focused on the miracles: the Red Sea becoming the Yellow Brick Road, fire escorting them by night and a cloud accompanying them by day, manna reflecting the morning sunrise and quail scampering into the camp at night. Instead they focused on their problems. They sketched pictures of Egypt, daydreamed of pyramids, and complained that life in the desert wasn't for them. They found something to complain about.

What about you? What are you looking at? The one fruit you

can't eat? Or the million you can? The manna or the misery? His plan or your problems? Each a gift or a grind?

> Finally, brethren, whatever things are true, whatever things are noble, whatever things are just, whatever things are pure, whatever things are lovely, whatever things are of good report, if there is any virtue and if there is anything praiseworthy— meditate on these things. (Philippians 4:8 NKJV)

This is more than a silver-lining attitude, more than seeing the cup as half full rather than half empty. This is an admission that unseen favorable forces populate and direct the affairs of humanity. When we see as God wants us to see, we see heaven's hand in the midst of sickness, Jesus working on a troubled youth, the Holy Spirit comforting a broken heart. We see not what is seen but what is unseen. We see with faith and not flesh, and since faith begets hope, we of all people are hope filled. For we know there is more to life than what meets the eye.

We see the "Christ; who will sustain you to the end" (1 Corinthians 1:7–8 RSV).

We believe that Jesus "who began a good work in you will carry it on to completion until the day of Christ Jesus" (Philippians 1:6 NIV).

We believe our Savior was serious when he said, "My Father is working still" (John 5:17 RSV).

And since God is working, the news anchor reports only some of the news and the doctor's prognosis offers only one opinion.

We look at people differently. We don't dismiss the kid with the learning disorder, the husband with the drinking problem, the preacher with the pride issue. We don't give up on people because we know that beneath the grate, beyond the rats, stands a stalk of grass, and we focus on it.

No one says it's easy to do. For the last five years my mother has been in an assisted-living facility not far from my house. The first few months I found it hard to see color amid the wrinkles, walkers, wheelchairs, and dentures. Each visit was a depressing reminder of my mom's failing health and fading memory.

Then I tried to practice the message of this book. Give every day a chance, even the days of old age. I began to spot blades of grass amid the people.

The loyalty of Elaine, also eighty-seven, who sits next to Mom at lunch. She cuts my mother's food so she can eat it.

The unsquashable enthusiasm of Lois, nearly eighty, who in spite of arthritis in both knees volunteers to pour the morning coffee every day.

The historical love of Joe and Barbara, celebrating seventy years, not of life but marriage. They take turns pushing each other in the wheelchair. Arthritis has enlarged the knuckles of her hand. We were no more than five minutes into the conversation, and he was gently lifting it toward me, expressing his concern.

Then there is Bob, left speechless and half paralyzed by a stroke. The picture on his door displays a younger Bob, smartly attired in military uniform; he used to give orders and command troops. Today his good hand steers the joystick of his wheelchair as he goes from table to table, wishing residents a good day by making the only sound he can: *Bmph.*

I used to see age, disease, and faded vigor. Now I see love, courage, and unflappable unselfishness.

And you? Does your world feel like General Risner's POW cell? Look long enough, hard enough, and it will. Even the garden of Eden looks gray to some. But it needn't look gray to you. Learn a lesson from the prisoner. Give every day a chance. Peer through the bricks, past the rats, to find the blade of grass. And once you find it, don't look anywhere else.

NOTES

Chapter 1: Every Day Deserves a Chance

1. My thanks to Judith Viorst and her children's book *Alexander and the Terrible, Horrible, No Good, Very Bad Day* (New York: Simon and Schuster, 1972).

Section 1: Saturate Your Day in His Grace

1. Gary L. Thomas, *Sacred Marriage: What If God Designed Marriage to Make Us Holy More than to Make Us Happy?* (Grand Rapids: Zondervan, 2000), 46–47.

Chapter 2: Mercy for Shame-Filled Days

1. Is this your first time to drink from the well of God's grace? If so, congratulations! You just entered into an eternity-altering relationship. "Whoever accepts and trusts the Son gets in on everything, life complete and forever!" (John 3:36). As you begin your new life, remember three Bs: baptism, Bible, belonging. Baptism demonstrates and celebrates our decision to follow Jesus. (See 1 Peter 3:21.) Regular Bible reading guides and anchors the soul. (See Hebrews 4:12.) Belonging to a church family engages us with God's children. (See Hebrews 10:25.) Ask God to lead you to a group of Christ followers who can celebrate your baptism, help you study the Bible, and serve as a church family.

Chapter 3: Gratitude for Ungrateful Days

1. Adapted from Rick Atchley, "When We All Get to Heaven" (sermon, Richland Hills Church of Christ, North Richland Hills, TX, May 25, 2005). Original source unknown.
2. Archibald Naismith, *2400 Outlines, Notes, Quotes, and Anecdotes for Sermons* (1967; repr., Grand Rapids: Baker Book House, 1991), #1063.
3. Alan Loy McGinnis, *The Balanced Life: Achieving Success in Work and Love* (Minneapolis: Augsburg Fortress, 1997), 56–57.

Chapter 4: Forgiveness for Bitter Days

1. Tripod, "Useless Information: Stuff You Never Needed to Know but Your Life Would Be Incomplete Without: The Collyer Brothers," http://earthdude1.tripod.com/collyer/collyer.html.
2. Antwone Quenton Fisher, "I Once Was Lost," *Reader's Digest*, July 2001, 81–86.

Chapter 5: Peace for Anxious Days

1. John Haggai, *How to Win Over Worry: A Practical Formula for Successful Living* (Eugene, OR: Harvest House Publishers, 1987), 14.
2. Haggai, *How to Win Over Worry*, 109.
3. Bob Russell, "Reinstated," *Favorite Stories from Bob Russell*, vol. 5, CD-ROM, Southeast Christian Church, Louisville, KY, 2005.
4. Charles Spurgeon, quoted in *The NIV Worship Bible*, New International Version (Dana Point, CA: Maranatha, 2000), 1302.
5. William Osler, quoted in Haggai, *How to Win Over Worry*, 109.
6. Eugene H. Peterson, *Run with the Horses: The Quest for Life at Its Best* (Madison, WI: InterVarsity Press, 1983), 115.

Chapter 6: Hope for Catastrophic Days

1. Mike Wise, "Pushed Beyond the Limit," *Washington Post*, August 30, 2004.
2. Romans 1:13; 1 Corinthians 11:3; 1 Thessalonians 4:13.
3. F. W. Boreham, *Life Verses: The Bible's Impact on Famous Lives,* vol. 2 (Grand Rapids: Kregel Publications, 1994), 114–55.

Chapter 8: Faith for Fear-Filled Days

1. Edward Beal, *1041 Sermon Illustrations, Ideas, and Expositions: Treasury of the Christian World*, ed. A. Gordon Nasby (1953; repr. Grand Rapids: Baker Book House, 1976), 109.

Chapter 9: Calling for Purposeless Days

1. My thanks to my friends John and Lisa Bentley, Michael Landon Jr., Shawn and Xochitl Hughes, and Daniel Sharp for allowing me to share their stories.
2. "A Real Death," *Birmingham (AL) Sunday Mercury*, December 17, 2000.

Chapter 10: Service for Fork-in-the-Road Days

1. "Miracle on Mount Everest," *Dateline NBC*, June 25, 2006, http://www.msnbc.msn.com/id/13543799.
2. Frederick Dale Bruner, *The Christbook: Matthew—A Commentary*, rev. and exp. ed. (Dallas: Word Publishing, 1987), 210.
3. "Miracle on Mount Everest," *Dateline NBC*.

Conclusion: The Blade of Uncommon Color

1. Robinson Risner, *The Passing of the Night: My Seven Years as a Prisoner of the North Vietnamese* (1973; repr. Duncanville: World Wide Printing, 2001), and a conversation with the author, February 24, 2004.
2. Risner, *The Passing of the Night* and a personal conversation.

DISCUSSION GUIDE

Chapter 1: *Every Day Deserves a Chance*

LOOK BACK

1. The cemetery dirt is still fresh, the pink slip still folded in your pocket, the other side of the bed still empty . . . who has a good day on these days? Most don't . . . but couldn't we try?

   A. Describe the most difficult day you had to endure in the past year. What made it so hard?

   B. Were you able to make it into a good day? If so, how?

2. God made this day, ordained this hard hour, designed the details of this wrenching moment. He isn't on holiday. He still holds the conductor's baton, sits in the cockpit, and occupies the universe's only throne.

   A. If a good God sits on the universe's only throne, why do you think he allows bad days?

   B. Do you believe that God ordained the hard hours of your life? Explain.

3. You no longer have yesterday. You do not yet have tomorrow. You have only today. *This* is the day the Lord has made. Live in it.

    A. Are you more prone to relive yesterday or to fear what might come tomorrow? Explain.

    B. What might you have to change about how you normally live in order to start living in *this* day?

4. Jesus doesn't use the term *day* very often in Scripture. But the few times he does use it provide a delightful formula for upgrading each of ours to blue-ribbon status. *Saturate your day in his grace. Entrust your day to his oversight. Accept his direction.*

    A. Which aspect of Jesus' formula for a good day is the hardest for you to follow? Why?

    B. Describe a time when you did saturate your day with his grace or did entrust your day to his oversight or did accept his direction for the day. How did it change the day?

LOOK UP

1. Read Psalm 118:24.

    A. Which day has the Lord made, according to this verse?

    B. Why not just say "the Lord makes all days"?

    C. If the Lord has made a day, what do you know about that day?

    D. Notice that the verse doesn't say "we *should* rejoice" but "let us rejoice" (NIV). What's the difference?

    E. What's the difference between rejoicing "in" something and rejoicing "for" it? How can this distinction be important?

2. Read Psalm 145:1–4.

    A. What does the writer say he will do every day?

    B. Why will he do this?

    C. What might be the effect on future generations?

    D. How would such a practice tend to change someone's outlook?

Chapter 2: Mercy for Shame-Filled Days

LOOK BACK

1. The thief hears the official language of Christ: grace. Undeserved. Unexpected. Grace. "Today you will join me in paradise."

   A. Why can we call grace the official language of Christ?

   B. How have you experienced the grace of Christ?

2. Paradise knows neither night nor second-class citizens. The thief enters the gate on Jesus' red carpet.

   A. What does Max mean by saying, "Paradise knows neither night nor second-class citizens"?

   B. Do you think it is fair that the "thief enters the gate on Jesus' red carpet"? Explain.

3. Execution hill becomes a mount of transfiguration.

   A. How did execution hill become a mount of transfiguration? Who was transfigured? How?

   B. How can your execution hill become your mount of transfiguration? How would this affect your approach to life?

4. You're soon nailed to the cross of your mistakes. Dumb mistakes. What do you see? Death. What do you feel? Shame. What do you hear? Ah, this is the question. What do you hear? Can you hear Jesus above the accusers? He promises, "Today you will join me in paradise."

   A. How can you begin to hear the voice of Jesus above the voices of your accusers and opponents?

   B. Why is it so important to hear the voice of Jesus after you've made some dumb mistake?

5. We are wrong. He is right. We sin. He is the Savior. We need grace. Jesus can give it.

   A. Do you find it difficult to tell God, "I am wrong. You are right"? Can you remember a specific occasion when you asked Jesus for his grace?

B. How do you recognize a grace-filled person?

LOOK UP

1. Read Luke 23:38–43.

   A. When you consider this scene, with whom do you identify? Why?

   B. What did the second criminal think of his own actions? What did he think of Jesus' behavior and character?

   C. What request did the second criminal make of Jesus?

   D. How did Jesus respond to this man?

2. Read 1 Peter 2:4–6.

   A. Who is the "living Stone" (NIV) in this passage? What does this name signify about him?

   B. What two different reactions to this person are described (v. 4)? What accounts for this difference?

   C. What promise is made in verse 5? Why is this important?

   D. What promise is made in verse 6? What does this mean for you?

Chapter 3: Gratitude for Ungrateful Days

LOOK BACK

1. The day of a dog. The day of a cat. One content, the other conniving. One at peace, the other at war. One grateful, the other grumpy. Same house. Same circumstances. Same master. Yet two entirely different attitudes. Which diary reads more like yours?

   A. How would you answer this question? Explain your answer.

   B. If you wanted to change how your diary reads, what might you have to do?

2. Gratitude is the firstborn child of grace, the appropriate response of the blessed. So appropriate, in fact, that its absence surprises Jesus.

    A. Why is gratitude the appropriate response of those who receive grace?

    B. Why do you think it surprises Jesus when those who have received his grace neglect to show gratitude in response? How often do you think you surprise Jesus in this way?

3. Gratitude lifts our eyes off the things we lack so we might see the blessings we possess. Nothing blows the winter out of the day like the Caribbean breeze of thankfulness.

    A. What blessings has God given you this week? This month? This year?

    B. On a scale of 1 (never) to 10 (continually), where would you rank yourself on your tendency to thank God for his blessings?

4. Need spice in your day? Thank God for every problem that comes down the pike.

    A. How does thanking God for a problem add spice to your day?

    B. Do you find it difficult to thank God for problems? Can you recall a specific problem in your life, thank God for it, and sincerely mean it? If so, how do you accomplish that?

5. Joni addressed the unhappy crowd. "I understand some of you don't like the chair in which you are sitting. Neither do I. But I have about a thousand handicapped friends who would gladly trade places with you in an instant."

    A. If you had been in the crowd that day, do you think you would have been numbered among the complainers? Explain.

    B. How do you react to Joni's words? Do they make you smile? Cringe? Feel grateful?

LOOK UP

1. Read Luke 17:11–19.

   A. What request did the ten men make of Jesus? What instructions did he give them in response?

   B. How many of the men complied with Jesus' instructions? What happened to them?

   C. One of the ten men responded differently from his companions. Why is it significant that this man is described as a Samaritan?

   D. How did the one man show his gratitude to Jesus? How did Jesus react to this show of gratitude?

   E. What question did Jesus ask? What most surprised him?

   F. Since the man had already been healed (v. 14), what is the point of Jesus' words in verse 19?

2. Read Colossians 3:15–17.

   A. What command appears in all three verses of the passage? What is significant about this?

   B. What is the connection between gratitude and giving thanks? Why are both necessary?

   C. Why do you think God insists that his children give thanks?

Chapter 4: Forgiveness for Bitter Days

LOOK BACK

1. Do you pack-rat pain? Amass offenses? Record slights? A tour of your heart might be telling.

   A. Why do you think so many of us tend to pack-rat pain?

   B. What would you uncover on a tour of your heart?

2. This guy is a grace rejecter. He never accepts the grace of the king. He leaves the throne room with a sly smirk, as one who

dodged a bullet, found a loophole, worked the system, pulled a fast one. He talked his way out of a jam. He bears the mark of the unforgiven—he refuses to forgive.

    A. How would you describe a grace rejecter?

    B. Why does a person's refusal to forgive others indicate a heart that has not accepted the forgiveness offered to him or her?

3. Apple trees bear apples, wheat stalks produce wheat, and forgiven people forgive people. Grace is the natural outgrowth of grace.

    A. Would you call yourself a forgiving person? Explain.

    B. How has God shown his grace to you lately? How have you shown that same grace to others?

4. Forgiveness does not mean approval. You aren't endorsing misbehavior. You are entrusting your offender to "Him who judges righteously."

    A. Why does offering forgiveness sometimes feel like giving approval? Why does forgiving someone feel as though you're letting the guy (or gal) off the hook?

    B. Do you find it hard or easy to entrust your offender to God, the righteous Judge? Explain.

LOOK UP

1. Read Matthew 18:21–35.

    A. What question prompted the parable Jesus told in this passage? What do you think Peter really wanted to know?

    B. Who are the main characters in the parable? Describe each one.

    C. What made the master so angry? What did he do because of his anger?

    D. What is the main point of the parable, according to Jesus (v. 35)?

E. What questions does this parable pose for you? Do you like this story? Explain.

2. Read 1 Peter 2:18–23.

A. What kind of example did Christ leave for us to follow, according to verse 21? How are we to follow in his steps in this area?

B. How is Jesus described in verse 22? Why is this important to Peter's point?

C. What did Jesus not do in response to unjust treatment (v. 23)? How did he respond instead?

D. How is God described in verse 23? Why is this important to remember when we suffer unjustly?

Chapter 5: Peace for Anxious Days

LOOK BACK

1. Worry is to joy what a Hoover vacuum cleaner is to dirt: might as well attach your heart to a happiness-sucker and flip the switch.

A. Would you describe yourself as a worrier? Explain.

B. How do you normally handle the worry that seeps into your heart?

2. This simple sentence unveils God's provision plan: *live one day at a time.*

A. What does it mean for you to live one day at a time? Do you usually manage this? Explain.

B. Describe an incident when God met your needs just in the nick of time.

3. Anxiety fades as our memory of God's goodness doesn't.

A. In what ways has God been good to you? How often do you recall his goodness, either out loud or in your mind?

B. Describe a time when you overcame a specific worry by focusing on a memory of how God had cared for you in the past.

4. No one can pray and worry at the same time. When we worry, we aren't praying. When we pray, we aren't worrying.

A. Is it true that no one can pray and worry at the same time? Explain.

B. Why does heartfelt, genuine prayer tend to overwhelm worry?

5. If God is enough for you, then you'll always have enough, because you'll always have God.

A. Is God enough for you? Explain.

B. Do you believe you'll always have God? Explain.

LOOK UP

1. Read Matthew 6:25–34.

A. What command does Jesus give in verse 25? What reason does he give for the command?

B. What illustration does Jesus give in verse 26? What questions does he ask (vv. 26–28)?

C. What further illustration does Jesus give in verse 28? What observation does he make in verse 29? What application does he make in verse 30?

D. What kinds of things do we tend to worry about (v. 31)? Why is it important not to follow the example of those mentioned in verse 32?

E. What does God know about our needs (v. 32)? Why is this important to remember?

F. What instructions does Jesus give us in verse 33? How can you personally follow these instructions?

G. What last reason does Jesus give for not worrying (v. 34)?

2. Read Hebrews 13:5–6.

    A. What command regarding money appears in verse 5? How can you comply with this command?

    B. What command regarding contentment is given in verse 5? How do you learn such contentment?

    C. What reason for these commands is given at the end of verse 5?

    D. When we focus on this reason, what takes place in our own hearts (v. 6)?

Chapter 6: Hope for Catastrophic Days

LOOK BACK

1. No one questions the fact of your misfortunes. But one would wisely question the wisdom of rehearsing them.

    A. Why is it unwise to mentally rehearse your misfortunes?

    B. What personal misfortune are you most likely to relive mentally? What generally happens when you allow yourself to wallow in that misfortune?

2. Rather than count the bricks of his prison, Paul plants a garden within it. He itemizes not the mistreatments of people but the faithfulness of God.

    A. How did Paul plant a garden within his prison walls? What did he do?

    B. How can you plant a garden within the prison walls that seem to hem you in? How might God take the evil that others do to you and use it for good instead?

3. Paul trusted the oversight of God. He didn't know why bad things happened. He didn't know how they would be resolved. But he knew who was in charge.

    A. If God is in charge, does that mean everything that happens pleases him?

B. What does it mean to you that God is in charge?

4. It's not easy to find joy in jail. Not easy to make the best of a derailed life. But God sends enough Paul and Joseph stories to convince us to give it a try.

　　A. Where is it most difficult, right now, for you to find joy? How could you give it a try?

　　B. What have you learned from the stories of Paul and Joseph that would encourage you to make the best of some derailed plans or delayed hopes?

5. Learn a lesson from Vanderlei de Lima: don't let the bumps in the race keep you from the award ceremony at its end.

　　A. Describe someone you know who is letting the bumps in the race distract him or her from finishing the race well.

　　B. What bumps in the race are threatening to keep you from the award ceremony? What can you do today to refocus your eyes on the end goal of the race?

LOOK UP

1. Read Philippians 1:12–21.

　　A. How did Paul assess his Roman imprisonment (v. 12)?

　　B. What groups benefited from Paul's incarceration (vv. 13–14)? How did they benefit?

　　C. What negative circumstance could have caused Paul much anguish while he was in jail (vv. 15–17)?

　　D. What did Paul choose to focus on while behind bars (v. 18)?

　　E. What kind of outlook for the future did Paul express (v. 19)?

　　F. For what specific thing did Paul hope (v. 20)?

　　G. How did Paul sum up his philosophy of life, regardless of what happened (v. 21)?

2. Read Hebrews 11:24–28.

　　A. What temptation did Moses face as an adult (v. 24)?

B. What choice did Moses make (v. 25)?

C. What gave Moses the strength to make this choice (v. 26)?

D. What kept Moses going, despite great difficulties, after he made this decision (v. 27)?

E. How did Moses' choice end up blessing a whole nation (v. 28)?

Chapter 7: Fuel for Depleted Days

LOOK BACK

1. The mistake of the disciples is not that they calculated the problem but that they calculated without Christ. In giving Jesus no chance, they gave their day no chance. They reserved a table for twelve at the Restaurant of the Rotten Day.

   A. Describe a time when you reserved a table at the Restaurant of the Rotten Day.

   B. How can Christ make a difference for you in whatever difficulties you're facing right now?

2. God is able to accomplish, provide, help, save, keep, subdue . . . He is able to do what you can't. He already has a plan.

   A. Do you believe that God already has a plan to help and provide for you? If not, why not? If so, how does your belief change the way you feel?

   B. What does God do for you that you can't do for yourself?

3. My first thought when I ran out of fuel was *How can I get this car to a gas pump?* Your first thought when you have a problem should be *How can I get this problem to Jesus?*

   A. How do you approach problems in your everyday life?

   B. What does it mean to you to give your problems to Jesus? How can you do this better in practice?

4. You're going to run out of gas. We all do. Next time the needle sits on the wrong side of empty, remember: the one who fed the crowds is a prayer away.

A. Tell how someone you know personally saw the miraculous hand of Jesus doing what that person could not do.

B. Do you think Jesus wants to work in your life as he worked in the lives of his disciples? Explain.

LOOK UP

1. Read Mark 6:30–44.

   A. What instructions did Jesus give his exhausted disciples in verse 31? Why did he give them these instructions?

   B. How did Jesus react to the crowds that tried to circumvent his instructions to his disciples (v. 34)? Why did he react in this way?

   C. What was the disciples' solution to the problem they faced (vv. 35–36)?

   D. How did Jesus respond to their suggestion (v. 37)?

   E. How did the disciples react to Jesus' instructions (v. 37)?

   F. How did Jesus involve his disciples in the solution (v. 41)?

   G. In your opinion, what did Jesus accomplish through this miracle?

2. Read 2 Corinthians 1:8–11.

   A. What did Paul want his friends to know about his circumstances (v. 8)?

   B. What did Paul mean by the "deadly peril" in verse 10 (NIV)?

   C. What hope for the future did Paul have (v. 10)?

   D. To whom did Paul look for assistance (v. 11)?

Chapter 8: Faith for Fear-Filled Days

LOOK BACK

1. Moments ago Jairus grand-marshaled the Hope Parade. Now he stands on the outside looking in and feels his fragile faith unravel. He looks toward his house and back at Christ and wonders afresh:

I wonder if he can. I wonder if he cares. I wonder if he'll come.

    A. Which of those three doubts—*I wonder if he can; I wonder if he cares; I wonder if he'll come*—do you struggle with the most? Explain.

    B. Why do you think Jesus sometimes allows your hope to rise and fall before he steps in to act decisively on your behalf?

2. To all who have stood where Jairus stood and asked what Jairus asked, Jesus says, "Don't be afraid; just believe."

    A. What situation in your life makes you most afraid right now?

    B. What does Jesus want you to believe in the situation you just described?

3. You will never go where God is not. You may be transferred, enlisted, commissioned, reassigned, or hospitalized, but—brand this truth on your heart—you can never go where God is not.

    A. Why is it impossible to go where God is not?

    B. Why does it so often feel as though God has left the building?

4. Give the day a chance. Believe he can. Believe he cares. Believe he comes. Don't be afraid. Just believe.

    A. How does belief tend to counteract fear?

    B. When you feel afraid, what most helps you to overcome that fear?

LOOK UP

1. Read Mark 5:21–43.

    A. What request did Jairus make of Jesus (v. 23)? What did his request indicate about his opinion of Jesus?

    B. What interruption caused Jairus to temporarily lose hope (vv. 24–34)? Why do you think Jesus permitted this interruption?

    C. What news further affected Jairus's hope (v. 35)? What did it reveal about the messengers' opinion of Jesus?

D. How did Jesus respond to the news these men brought (v. 36)? Why did he focus his attention on Jairus and not on the men who brought the message?

E. Who declared the real truth in verses 38–39? How did the people react to the real truth (v. 40)?

F. How did the story turn out (vv. 41–43)? How did the people react to this (v. 42)? How did Jesus react to the same thing (v. 43)? Why?

2. Read Isaiah 51:12–15.

A. Who is speaking in verse 12? Why does this make a big difference?

B. What question is asked in verse 12? What problem does the question uncover?

C. What does fear of others tend to do in our hearts (v. 13)? How does God suggest that we counteract this tendency?

D. What promise does God give his people in verses 12–15? On what is this promise based?

Chapter 9: Calling for Purposeless Days

LOOK BACK

1. The cross is God's tool of redemption, instrument of salvation— proof of his love for people. To take up the cross, then, is to take up Christ's burden for the people of the world.

A. How does the cross prove God's love for people?

B. In what ways can Christ's followers take up his burden for the people of the world?

2. What is your task? What is your unique call, assignment, mission?

A. Describe when and how you learned that you had gifts God could use.

B. How can you use your gifts to share God's love for the world?

3. In what directions has God taken you? What needs has God revealed to you? What abilities has God given to you?

A. How would you respond to Max's questions?

B. How can you model your response for your children, your grandchildren, or those in your sphere of influence?

4. While none of us is called to carry the sin of the world (Jesus did that), all of us can carry a burden for the world.

A. Have you experienced a meaningful moment while caring for "the world"? Explain.

B. How does this kind of burden not weigh you down or make you fretful?

5. Something stirs you. Some call brings energy to your voice, conviction to your face, and direction to your step. Isolate and embrace it. Nothing gives a day a greater chance than a good wallop of passion.

A. How has your burden for the world affected your spiritual walk?

B. What have you learned from actively caring for others?

LOOK UP

1. Read Luke 9:23–25.

A. What does it mean to "come after" Jesus (v. 23 NIV)? What does it mean to deny oneself? What does it mean to take up a cross? How often must this be done? What does it mean to follow Jesus?

B. What happens to those who try to save their own lives (v. 24)? What happens to those who lose their lives for Jesus' sake?

C. What question does Jesus ask in verse 25? In what way is this a great question to ask every day of your life?

2. Read Ephesians 2:10.

A. Whose workmanship are you? What does this mean for you?

B. In whom are you created? What does this mean for you?

C. For what are you created? What does this mean for you?

D. How can you be certain that your Spirit-led efforts will not be in vain? How can the truth of this verse increase your confidence in living for God?

Chapter 10: *Service for Fork-in-the-Road Days*

LOOK BACK

1. Would we surrender ambition to save someone else? Set aside our dreams to rescue another climber? Turn our backs on our personal mountaintops so someone else might live?

   A. How would you answer the questions above?

   B. Describe a time when someone sacrificed his or her plans in order to help you grow or succeed or get ahead.

2. Behold the most surprising ingredient of a great day: self-denial.

   A. What does "self-denial" mean to you?

   B. Does self-denial mean that you refuse to consider your own legitimate needs? Explain.

3. The sweetest satisfaction lies not in climbing your own Everest but in helping other climbers.

   A. Describe how you felt the last time you helped someone else climb his or her Mount Everest.

   B. Why do you think it gives us a thrill to genuinely help someone else who needs our help?

4. Want to snatch a day from the manacles of boredom? Do overgenerous deeds, acts beyond reimbursement. Kindness without compensation. Do a deed for which you cannot be repaid.

   A. If you have ever done a deed for which you could not be repaid, describe it. What happened?

    B. How does lavish generosity snatch a day from the manacles of boredom?

5. We're important but not essential, valuable but not indispensable. We have a part in the play, but we are not the main act. A song to sing, but we are not the featured voice. God is.

    A. What's the difference between important and essential, valuable and indispensable? Why do we need to keep these differences in mind?

    B. How is God essential to your life? How is he indispensable? If you could not pray for a whole year, what in your life would change?

LOOK UP

1. Read John 13:1–17.

    A. What is important about the timing of this incident (v. 1)?

    B. How did Jesus show his disciples the full extent of his love (v. 1)?

    C. What empowered Jesus to do what he was about to do (v. 3)? How can the same things empower us?

    D. What did Jesus do (vv. 4–5)? Why was this totally unexpected?

    E. How did Peter react to Jesus' actions (vv. 6–8)? How did Jesus respond to Peter? What did he mean?

    F. What lesson did Jesus want to teach his followers through this incident (vv. 12–15)?

    G. For whom does Jesus reserve a blessing, according to verse 17? Do you expect to receive this blessing? Explain.

2. Read Luke 14:12–14.

    A. What instructions does Jesus give in verse 12? Why does he give these instructions?

B. What further instruction does Jesus give in verse 13?

C. What promise does Jesus give in verse 14? When will the promise be fulfilled? Why is this important to keep in mind?

Conclusion: *The Blade of Uncommon Color*

LOOK BACK

1. Do you know the tint of a colorless world? If so, do what Risner did. Go on a search. Crowbar the grate from your cell, and stick your head out. Fix your eyes on a color outside your cell.

   A. What in your life seems most colorless?

   B. On what color outside your cell can you focus?

2. We all make daily decisions. Do we set our eyes on the gray harshness or search for the blade of a different color?

   A. Where do you most often choose to set your eyes? On the color or the grayness?

   B. What tends to happen when you focus on the gray harshness? What tends to happen when you focus on the color?

3. If you look hard enough, long enough, you'll find something to complain about.

   A. Do you tend to look for the negative or the positive?

   B. How often do you find yourself complaining to others?

4. Even the garden of Eden looks gray to some. But it needn't look gray to you. Learn a lesson from the prisoner. Give every day a chance. Peer through the bricks, past the rats, to find the blade of grass.

   A. How could the garden of Eden look gray to someone?

   B. Are you giving every day a chance? Are you giving today a chance? Explain.

LOOK UP

1. Read Colossians 3:1–3.
    A. To whom is this passage addressed (v. 1)? Does this describe you? Explain.
    B. What instructions are given in verses 1 and 2? How can you do this on a daily, practical basis?
    C. What reason does Paul give for these instructions (v. 3)?
2. Read Philippians 4:8.
    A. What truths can you ponder?
    B. What noble or honorable things can you dwell on?
    C. What things are right or just that can strengthen you?
    D. What things are pure that you can focus on?
    E. What lovely things can equip you to serve God well?
    F. What things are admirable or of good report that can inspire you?
    G. What excellent and praiseworthy things can you think about today to give you a proper perspective?

CHANGE YOUR DAY, CHANGE YOUR LIFE

A Thirty-Day Journey

Prepared by literary developer Lance Wubbels,
Koechel Peterson & Associates, Inc., Minneapolis, MN

DAY CHANGER 1

Saturate Your Day in His Grace

> This is the day the LORD has made;
> We will rejoice and be glad in it. (Psalm 118:24 NKJV)

Entrust Your Day to His Oversight

Dear Lord, help these words sink in. You made this day. You ordained this hour. You designed the details of this very moment. You never take a vacation. You still occupy the highest throne and direct this day's affairs. Whatever this day brings, I receive it from your hands. Help me to embrace it as your day, to rejoice and be glad in it. In Jesus' name I pray, amen.

Accept His Direction

Rejoice *in* this day. Paul rejoiced *in* prison. David wrote psalms *in* the wilderness. Jesus prayed *in* the garden of pain. Resolve to give this day a shot. Choose to give it a fair shake and the best possible chance. Trust more. Stress less. Amplify gratitude. Mute grumbling. Build your life one good day at a time!

Identify one tough area of your life, and choose to rejoice in it today.

....

....

Saturate Your Day in His Grace

> "Show me, O LORD, my life's end
>> and the number of my days;
>> let me know how fleeting is my life.
>> You have made my days a mere handbreadth;
>> the span of my years is as nothing before you.
>> Each man's life is but a breath." (Psalm 39:4–5 NIV)

Entrust Your Day to His Oversight

Lord, today is before me. Yesterday is gone and cannot be retrieved. Help me accept that I can't alter it or improve it and that there's no reason to fret over it. Remind me that tomorrow isn't yet here and that I don't need to worry about what might be. I want to live my life to the fullest today . . . in this present moment . . . with all my heart. In Jesus' name I pray, amen.

Accept His Direction

Be present today. Live in the moments you have. Dwelling in the past will only sabotage today's joys. You'll have what you need tomorrow. Give today a chance. Be present in the moments you have, and fill your day with God.

Identify something in the last week that caused regret,
ask forgiveness if needed, and then let it go.

....

....

Saturate Your Day in His Grace

"If you don't go all the way with me, through thick and thin, you don't deserve me. If your first concern is to look after yourself, you'll never find yourself. But if you forget about yourself and look to me, you'll find both yourself and me." (Matthew 10:38–39)

Entrust Your Day to His Oversight

Father, I want to follow Jesus, so help me learn what it means to forget about myself. Thank you that your grace has erased my guilt and that your lordship of my life removes fear. In times of confusion, give me direction. I accept your direction and your will for my life. In Jesus' name I pray, amen.

Accept His Direction

If you wonder what your life is about, remember that it is to follow Jesus one day at a time. Train your eyes to look toward him every moment of the day, and you'll find the joy and peace that come only from having Christ at the center of your life.

The first time today that you begin to think about your own wants and needs, turn your thoughts toward gratitude for a gift God has given you.

Saturate Your Day in His Grace

Then he [one of the criminals hanging on a cross next to Jesus] said, "Jesus, remember me when you enter your kingdom."

He said, "Don't worry, I will. Today you will join me in paradise." (Luke 23:42–43)

Entrust Your Day to His Oversight

Lord, I am amazed by the miracle of your forgiveness. Your grace transforms my shame into forgiveness. Your mercy permeates every moment of my life. You open the door to my future and cover my moments with love. In Jesus' name I pray, amen.

Accept His Direction

The official language of Jesus Christ is grace. We don't deserve it, and we have no right to expect it. But he covers our shame-filled days with grace like a tidal wave, washing our guilt away. We all sin. We all need grace. And Jesus freely gives it. He'll take your guilt if you'll ask him. Isn't this a good time to do so?

With Christ as your example, choose to forgive someone who has wronged you. Show that person undeserved, unexpected grace.

....

....

DAY CHANGER 5

Saturate Your Day in His Grace

All praise to God, the Father of our Lord Jesus Christ, who has blessed us with every spiritual blessing in the heavenly realms because we are united with Christ. (Ephesians 1:3 NLT)

Entrust Your Day to His Oversight

Father, because of your Son and the richness of your mercies, I am alive today. I can walk in the light and live free of the chains of sin. Apart from Jesus, I would be without hope and without you, the living God. All praise to you for uniting me with Jesus. How can I ever praise you enough? In his name I pray, amen.

Accept His Direction

The key to relishing more of your day is to begin with God's grace. As you accept his forgiveness, your gripes and groans will become gratitude. Yes, gratitude. Gratitude is the offspring of grace, the fitting response of the blessed.

Write down three blessings that come from being united with Christ. Tell God how thankful you are for each of them.

....

....

DAY CHANGER 6

Saturate Your Day in His Grace

    Always be joyful. Pray continually, and give thanks what-
ever happens. That is what God wants for you in Christ
Jesus. (1 Thessalonians 5:16–18 NCV)

Entrust Your Day to His Oversight

Father, I am surrounded by a garden of grace reflecting your love.
I choose to lift my eyes off the weeds in my life, which get so
much of my attention, and to put my focus on your grace. I thank
you in advance for whatever fills today, whether weeds or flowers.
In Jesus' name I pray, amen.

Accept His Direction

Measure the gifts of God. Collect your blessings. Catalog his
kindnesses. Assemble your reasons for gratitude and recite them.
Gratitude is always an option. Make gratitude your default emotion, and you'll find yourself giving thanks for everything. Give
thanks whatever happens.

Identify three trouble spots throughout your day,
and thank God for them as they arise.

....

....

Saturate Your Day in His Grace

> We take every thought captive so that it is obedient to Christ.
> (2 Corinthians 10:5 GOD'S WORD)

Entrust Your Day to His Oversight

Lord Jesus, there's a battle going on in my mind all the time, and it's so easy to allow negative thoughts to fill me with doubt, bitterness, and fear. I recognize that my thoughts run my life and that I control those thoughts. Help me choose to heed positive thoughts that are true to your Word instead of negative ideas. In Jesus' name I pray, amen.

Accept His Direction

Be careful which thoughts you allow to dwell in your mind. Positive thoughts strengthen you. They remind you of your place in the kingdom of God and build hope in your heart. Ponder the positives. Dwell on the delightful. Take every thought captive, and make it obey Jesus.

Which thoughts do you need to take captive today? Identify them, and remind yourself of truths that bring hope and strength.

....

....

Saturate Your Day in His Grace

"He [a servant who owed the king a great sum] couldn't pay, so his master ordered that he be sold—along with his wife, his children, and everything he owned—to pay the debt.

"But the man fell down before his master and begged him, 'Please, be patient with me, and I will pay it all.' Then his master was filled with pity for him, and he released him and forgave his debt." (Matthew 18:25–27 NLT)

Entrust Your Day to His Oversight

Father, today I celebrate your sheer generosity. I was swimming in a Pacific Ocean of sin debt. My personal payout was unachievable. But you saw my condition and pardoned me. May I never lose the wonder of your amazing grace. In Jesus' name I pray, amen.

Accept His Direction

God forgives the unforgivable. He offers titanic forgiveness. Accept that grace today. Take his pure gift into your heart, and rejoice in it. Believe it's true. Sing and celebrate. Host a Thanksgiving Day parade. And as you've received multimillion-dollar forgiveness, be a multimillion-dollar forgiver of others.

Have you committed a sin you secretly believe is unforgivable? Ask for forgiveness today, confident that your debt has already been paid. Don't wait.

Saturate Your Day in His Grace

> Then Peter came to him and asked, "Lord, how often should I forgive someone who sins against me? Seven times?"
>
> "No, not seven times," Jesus replied, "but seventy times seven!" (Matthew 18:21–22 NLT)

Entrust Your Day to His Oversight

Lord, you have forgiven me much. The hurts that I have endured are minuscule compared to the things for which you have forgiven me. I refuse to be a victim to hurts. I hand these situations over to you and leave them in your hands. I choose forgiveness. Because you first loved me, I will seek to love others today, forgiving them with your help. In Jesus' name I pray, amen.

Accept His Direction

Hoarding hurts in your heart destroys joy. Instead, claim the peace and joy that God offers, and follow his example. Choose to forgive others. The grace-given give grace. Forgiven people forgive people. The mercy-marinated drip mercy. Grace is the natural outgrowth of grace.

Single out a hurt that you've been hoarding, and make a conscious choice to forgive the perpetrator. Then tell that person you've forgiven him or her.

....

....

Saturate Your Day in His Grace

> God knew what he was doing from the very beginning. He decided from the outset to shape the lives of those who love him along the same lines as the life of his Son. (Romans 8:29)

Entrust Your Day to His Oversight

Father, I am thrilled that you desire to make me more like Jesus today. Help me understand what that means. I depend on the power of your Spirit to shape my life along the same lines as Jesus'. Teach me to serve others, to freely give of myself for others, and to do what is right, as Jesus did. Make me into the image of Jesus. In his name I pray, amen.

Accept His Direction

God's agenda for your day is to make you more like his Son. Jesus felt no guilt; God wants you to feel no guilt. Jesus had no bad habits; God wants to do away with yours. Jesus faced fears and even death with courage; God wants you to do the same. This is God's ultimate goal for your life, and he will faithfully bring it to pass.

Pinpoint one trait of Jesus, and try to live out that trait today.

....

....

Saturate Your Day in His Grace

"Give us day by day our daily bread." (Luke 11:3 NKJV)

Entrust Your Day to His Oversight

Lord, I have experienced your love and goodness, and yet anxiety often plagues my steps. You have resources I know nothing about, solutions outside my reality, provisions beyond my possibility. I remember the miracle of your salvation, and I come confidently to your throne, knowing you will give me all I need for this day. In Jesus' name I pray, amen.

Accept His Direction

Live one day at a time. You don't have wisdom for tomorrow's problems. But you will tomorrow. You don't have resources for tomorrow's needs. But you will tomorrow. You don't have courage for tomorrow's challenges. But you will when tomorrow comes. God meets daily needs daily.

What worries are you borrowing from tomorrow?
Capture these fears, and thank God for what
he has given you to meet today's needs.

....

....

Saturate Your Day in His Grace

"Give your entire attention to what God is doing right now, and don't get worked up about what may or may not happen tomorrow. God will help you deal with whatever hard things come up when the time comes." (Matthew 6:34)

Entrust Your Day to His Oversight

Father, I will delight in you and find my joy in you. I will find strength for today by not fretting over tomorrow's problems. In you I find enough for today, and no one can separate me from you, so I always have enough. Thank you for all you are doing in my life today. I will be content and grateful for your provision. In Jesus' name I pray, amen.

Accept His Direction

Pray more. Prayer and worry are mutually exclusive; you can't do them at the same time. When we worry, we aren't praying. When we pray, we aren't worrying. "You will keep him in perfect peace, whose mind is stayed on You, because he trusts in You" (Isaiah 26:3 NKJV). When you pray, you put your mind on Christ, resulting in peace. Bow your head and banish anxiety.

Identify a regular activity that often causes anxiety (e.g., paying bills, dropping off kids at school), and commit to surrounding that time with prayer today.

....

....

Saturate Your Day in His Grace

> And we know that God causes everything to work together for the good of those who love God and are called according to his purpose for them. (Romans 8:28 NLT)

Entrust Your Day to His Oversight

Lord, I've read how Paul was beaten, lied about, storm tossed, rejected, neglected, and imprisoned. Yet he still sang a song of joy. It is possible to find unbridled joy in the midst of extraordinary unfairness, unkindness, and pain. I trust that you'll take the tangled threads of my life today and make them all work together for good. In Jesus' name I pray, amen.

Accept His Direction

You know who is in charge of your day and your life. No matter what happens, God is in control of this day, so you can rejoice in the highs and find hope in the lows. You may not know why the lows hit when they do or how they will be resolved, but you can trust the One in control. Knowing who's in charge counterbalances the mysteries of why and how. Find joy; make the best of your day. Trust God.

Recall a time when you struggled to understand the whys of your situation but now you can see how God used that in your life. Rely on that memory to fortify you through tough days.

....

....

Saturate Your Day in His Grace

Don't shuffle along, eyes to the ground, absorbed with the things right in front of you. Look up, and be alert to what is going on around Christ—that's where the action is. See things from *his* perspective. (Colossians 3:2)

Entrust Your Day to His Oversight

Lord Jesus, even during the Friday of your extreme suffering, you spoke repeatedly to or about your Father. It was true of your entire life; you talked to or thought about the Father all day long. So I take my eyes off myself and look up to you today. Help me see the invisible and rest my life in your hands. In Jesus' name I pray, amen.

Accept His Direction

God's love is the remedy to your suffering. His acceptance the antidote to being rejected. He holds open his arms of love to you, a haven in the uncertainty of this world. When problems disturb you, follow the resolve of Paul: "We don't look at the troubles we can see now; rather, we fix our gaze on things that cannot be seen" (2 Corinthians 4:18 NLT). Look to Christ for love and acceptance beyond measure.

Tell a friend about something good God
is doing in your life right now.

....

....

Saturate Your Day in His Grace

Throw the whole weight of your anxieties upon him, for you are his personal concern. (1 Peter 5:7 Phillips)

Entrust Your Day to His Oversight

Father, your Word tells me that you are able to provide me with every blessing in abundance and to help me through every temptation and test. I unload my worries on you, knowing you can do what I can't, and I leave them in your hands. Thank you for your overflowing love and care. In Jesus' name I pray, amen.

Accept His Direction

God is able. He can do what you can't, and he already has a plan (John 6:6). The next time life's problems arise, your first thought should be *How can I give this to Jesus?* Confess your weakness, and ask for help. God's solution is a prayer away!

> *Name at least one area of your life where you are weak today. Ask God to be strong where you aren't and to let his love overflow into this area.*

....

....

DAY CHANGER 16

Saturate Your Day in His Grace

> When he [Jairus] saw Jesus, he fell to his knees, beside himself as he begged, "My dear daughter is at death's door. Come and lay hands on her so she will get well and live." Jesus went with him, the whole crowd tagging along, pushing and jostling him. (Mark 5:22–24)

Entrust Your Day to His Oversight

Lord Jesus, why do I doubt you when I know you gave your life for me? Why do I wonder if you care about my needs? In the push and shove of this day, enter my life and help me know that you are coming to meet me at every point of need. You know the best way to help. In Jesus' name I pray, amen.

Accept His Direction

Jesus' instant willingness to help this father demonstrates that Jesus *can*, *cares*, and will *come*. Jesus *can* help you. Jesus *does* care. Jesus *is* coming. Your need may be your marriage, your career, your future, or a friend. Don't try to dictate the terms of his help or his coming, but trust he is on the way.

When has God shown up in your life in an astounding way?
Write down how your story parallels that of the father in Mark 5.
Thank God for demonstrating his love for you by showing up.

....

....

Saturate Your Day in His Grace

> While Jesus was still speaking, some men came from the house of Jairus, the synagogue ruler. "Your daughter is dead," they said. "Why bother the teacher any more?"
>
> Ignoring what they said, Jesus told the synagogue ruler, "Don't be afraid; just believe." (Mark 5:35–36 NIV)

Entrust Your Day to His Oversight

Father, fear pillages so much from my days. Even when I know you're right by my side, some things in my life make absolutely no sense to me and trigger doubt. Speak this word into my heart today: "Don't be afraid; just believe." I need it to help get me through. Lord, I do believe. In Jesus' name I pray, amen.

Accept His Direction

Believe. Jesus comes to the houses of people like Jairus and to your house. He just asks you to believe. To believe that his heart of compassion is bigger than your trials. That his heart of love extends beyond your line of sight. That he is greater than what lies ahead. Believe that Jesus is able to help and that he comes to all. He speaks to all. Just *believe.*

Look at what you wrote down for Day Changer 16. Ask God to show up in another trial of your life in his timing.

....

....

Saturate Your Day in His Grace

> "I am with you always, even to the end of the age." (Matthew 28:20 NKJV)

Entrust Your Day to His Oversight

Lord Jesus, I want to follow your example. You faced the cross. I want to face my fears with the same kind of faith. When I face the unknown today, things I don't understand, my hope is anchored to you and your presence with me. I will joyfully walk forward, knowing you are with me. In Jesus' name I pray, amen.

Accept His Direction

The presence of fear does not mean you have no faith. Fear visits everyone. But make your fear a visitor and not a resident. Mark this down: you will never go where God is not. You may move to the ends of the earth, the top of the world, or the South Pole. God is still there, still with you.

Write Matthew 28:20 on a note card, and tuck it into your wallet or purse. When you feel as if you're doing life alone today, read that note card, and remember God's promise to you.

Saturate Your Day in His Grace

> "And he arose and came to his father. But when he was still a great way off, his father saw him and had compassion, and ran and fell on his neck and kissed him." (Luke 15:20 NKJV)

Entrust Your Day to His Oversight

Father, the thought of you running toward me is overwhelming, and yet I know it's true. Your heart of love is always overflowing. I leave behind those things that would keep me from feasting in your house and turn toward you today. I know I am on the pathway that leads to your embrace. In Jesus' name I pray, amen.

Accept His Direction

Brighten your day by envisioning God running toward you. When the teen walks away from the party, the ladder-climbing executive pushes back from the desk, or the materialist gives away his stuff, God can't sit still. Heaven's throne room echoes with the sound of slapping sandals and pounding feet, and angels watch in silence as God embraces his child. Turn toward God, and he runs toward you.

Pinpoint at least one way that you need to
turn toward God today. Do that now.

....

....

Saturate Your Day in His Grace

> Like an open book, you watched me grow from conception
>   to birth;
>   all the stages of my life were spread out before you,
> The days of my life all prepared
>   before I'd even lived one day. (Psalm 139:16)

Entrust Your Day to His Oversight

Father, it's hard for me to wrap my mind around your perspective on my life. It humbles me that you have written me into your great story and that you have a role for me to play today. Be Lord of my life, and show me what you have prepared me to fulfill. May I bring glory to you. In Jesus' name I pray, amen.

Accept His Direction

Your life is significant. When God wrote his story, he wrote you into it. No assignment too small, no lines too brief. He has a definite direction for your life. Fulfill it and enjoy fulfillment. Play the part God prepared for you, and get ready to see some great days.

Write down at least two of your roles that sometimes feel insignificant. Then note one way that each of these roles serves God.

....

....

Saturate Your Day in His Grace

Then Jesus said to all the people:

If any of you want to be my followers, you must forget about yourself. You must take up your cross each day and follow me. (Luke 9:23 CEV)

Entrust Your Day to His Oversight

Lord, it's so easy to think of my cross as a personal hassle that no one wants. Today I want to see it as the burden for the world that you've placed in my life, the good weight that you said is light to carry. This is a sweet day because I purpose to put my passions behind my gifts and talents and make a difference in the world. In Jesus' name I pray, amen.

Accept His Direction

The cross is God's tool of redemption and the ultimate proof of his love for people, and he's asked us to carry that same love for the world. To take up the cross is to take up your individual calling to show God's love to the world. And what better way to do that than through your God-designed passions. Enlist your gifts and talents. Using those God-given talents will lighten the weight of your cross.

Make note of a way you can use your gifts to show at least one person in the world how much God loves him or her. Try to do that today.

....

....

Saturate Your Day in His Grace

The Lord has assigned to each his task. (1 Corinthians 3:5 NIV)

Entrust Your Day to His Oversight

Father, just as Moses' childhood experiences prepared him to stand before Pharaoh, my past is no accident either. Give me wisdom to know the mission you have for my life and how I can use all that you've put into me to be effective in reaching out to others. Help me run the particular race you have set before me. In Jesus' name I pray, amen.

Accept His Direction

What is your God-designed task? You know you have one. A unique call. An original mission. Tally up the experiences unique to you—your culture and the lifestyles you've been exposed to. Your past is a signpost to your future, as it was for Moses, David, and Paul. What are your burdens? What needs has God revealed to you? What makes your heart race and your blood pump? Nothing gives a day a greater chance than a good wallop of passion.

> *Add to your list from Day Changer 21. Jot down one way you can use your passions to show God's love to someone with a physical, spiritual, or emotional need. Then do it!*

....

....

Saturate Your Day in His Grace

> Christ has given each of us special abilities—whatever he wants us to have out of his rich storehouse of gifts. (Ephesians 4:7 TLB)

Entrust Your Day to His Oversight

Lord Jesus, thank you for the special abilities you've given me. I ask you to help me carefully explore and test who I am and all you've put inside me. I want to be the very best I can be, for your honor and glory. In your name I pray, amen.

Accept His Direction

What comes easy to you? You excel at something and do so with comparatively little effort. What stirs you and brings energy to your voice, conviction to your face, and direction to your step? Identify your spiritual *DNA—direction, need, ability.* You at your best. God has given you special abilities. Identify and use them!

Revisit your list from Day Changers 21 and 22. Look for a trend in the way you reach out to others. Does this reveal a special ability? Write down two ways you can use this ability to show God's love to the world.

....

....

Saturate Your Day in His Grace

> Pray in the Spirit at all times with all kinds of prayers, asking for everything you need. To do this you must always be ready and never give up. Always pray for all God's people. (Ephesians 6:18 NCV)

Entrust Your Day to His Oversight

Lord Jesus, I ask you to inject your passion into me today. You loved us so much that you gave your life to save us. Give me your heart for people. Help me pray fervently for others. Help me speak to others in a manner consistent with the way you did. Help me care as you care for me. In your name I pray, amen.

Accept His Direction

Pray for every person you pass. Waiting in line? Stopped in traffic? Take the time to pray for those around you, whether you know them or not. *Stir* spiritual dialogue. At the right time, with the right heart, ask your friends and family, "What is your view of Jesus?" or "What do you think happens when we die?" *Love* because God loves. People can be tough to love. Love them anyway.

Pray for three saints and three strangers throughout your day.

....

....

Saturate Your Day in His Grace

"Whoever compels you to go one mile, go with him two."
(Matthew 5:41 NKJV)

Entrust Your Day to His Oversight

Lord, my nature is to bristle whenever an unreasonable or unjust demand is made on my life. I want to serve others, to forgive others, and to consider others better than myself with joy and grace, but I can't do it on my own. Help me shock someone today by serving well past the second mile. And help me smile and really mean it while I'm at it. In Jesus' name I pray, amen.

Accept His Direction

Jesus introduced the first-century Jews to a new reaction to the Roman oppressors: Serve the ones who hate you, forgive the ones who hurt you, and join the Society of the Second Mile. Take the lowest place, not the highest. Retaliate, not in kind but in kindness. Give more than requested or demanded, and do so with joy and grace! Discover the secret of joy found in the extra effort. The sweetest satisfaction lies in helping others.

*Listen closely today. When you hear a request for
help, be quick to offer more than is asked.*

....

....

DAY CHANGER 26

Saturate Your Day in His Grace

> Mary came in with a jar of very expensive aromatic oils, anointed and massaged Jesus' feet, and then wiped them with her hair. The fragrance of the oils filled the house. (John 12:3)

Entrust Your Day to His Oversight

Father, help me follow Mary's example and be an extravagant giver, even if others criticize me as they did her. Show me the people and the places of service that you want me to pour my life into, and help me do it freely and joyfully. May the sweet aroma of your Son fill my offering. In Jesus' name I pray, amen.

Accept His Direction

Jesus said it's better to give than to receive (Acts 20:35). Have you found that true? Shock someone with kindness without compensation. Give something outlandish, and you'll take a day from monotonous to monumental.

Do a deed for which you cannot be repaid.

....

....

Saturate Your Day in His Grace

But we see Jesus, who for a short time was made lower than the angels. And now he is wearing a crown of glory and honor because he suffered and died. And by God's grace, he died for everyone. (Hebrews 2:9 NCV)

Entrust Your Day to His Oversight

Lord, Moses was one of history's foremost leaders, yet your Word states that he was more humble than anyone else on the face of the earth. Today I want only to be numbered among the servants of your kingdom. Help me humble myself before you, take up my cross, and follow in your footsteps. In Jesus' name I pray, amen.

Accept His Direction

Moses chose humility. Jesus chose the servants' quarters. Can't we? We've been given a part to play in God's production—but we're not the stars. God is. He started it all, sustains it all, and will bring it all to a glorious climax. You have the rare privilege of following the greatest Servant of all.

Think about one characteristic of the best servants you know.
Begin today to incorporate that trait into your life.

....

....

DAY CHANGER 28

Saturate Your Day in His Grace
> Teach us how short our lives really are
> so that we may be wise. (Psalm 90:12 NCV)

Entrust Your Day to His Oversight

Father, it's good to be reminded that our days are numbered and that today I am one day closer to death. This, in fact, could be my last day, for all I know. So help me live to the fullest, treasure the people in my life, and love and forgive with such passion that there will be no regrets if this is my last day. In Jesus' name I pray, amen.

Accept His Direction

If today were your last day of life, how would you spend it? Would you do what you're doing now? Or would you love more, give more, forgive more? Then do so! Forgive and give as if it were your last opportunity. Love like there's no tomorrow, and if tomorrow comes, love again.

Name one thing you will do today to live without regrets.

....

....

Saturate Your Day in His Grace

"Your eyes are windows into your body. If you open your eyes wide in wonder and belief, your body fills up with light. If you live squinty-eyed in greed and distrust, your body is a dank cellar. If you pull the blinds on your windows, what a dark life you will have!" (Matthew 6:22–23)

Entrust Your Day to His Oversight

Lord, Adam and Eve were surrounded by all they would have ever needed, and yet they set their eyes on the one thing they couldn't have. The followers of Moses could have focused on all the miracles you did, and yet they complained about perceived unfulfilled needs. Help me see the wonder of all your goodness in my life and live forever grateful. In Jesus' name I pray, amen.

Accept His Direction

Jesus is interested in the eyes of your heart—your attitude, your outlook, your vision for your life. So set your eyes on all the goodness of God. Do you see how he has dressed the fields with wildflowers? Do you feel the warmth of the sun and the chill of the rain? He's provided all this for you, and he didn't stop there. He sent his Son. Put your eyes on gifts from above.

Make note of three ways God is showing his grace in your life.

....

....

Saturate Your Day in His Grace

There has never been the slightest doubt in my mind that the God who started this great work in you would keep at it and bring it to a flourishing finish on the very day Christ Jesus appears. (Philippians 1:6)

Entrust Your Day to His Oversight

Father, I believe that Jesus will sustain me until the end and complete the good work he is doing in my life today. I believe in you even though I can't see you, and I believe you are working in my life. Give me eyes that see other people and situations from the perspective of faith, and make my life a blessing. In Jesus' name I pray, amen.

Accept His Direction

This is more than a silver-lining attitude, more than seeing the cup as half full. This is an admission that you need God's help to make it through even the best days. It's total reliance on the One who is faithful to continue his work in you day after day. We, of all people, are hope filled, because we know there is more to life than just today's struggles.

Building on your list from Day Changer 29, identify ways that God's continued work gives you hope for today and every day.

....

....